UNCOMMON OBDURATE:

THE SEVERAL PUBLIC CAREERS

OF J. F. W. DesBARRES

Presumed to be J. F. W. DesBarres after middle age.
Copy of a watercolor sketch.
Courtesy of Public Archives of Canada.

UNCOMMON OBDURATE:

The Several Public Careers

of J. F. W. DesBarres

By G. N. D. EVANS

Peabody Museum of Salem, Massachusetts, U. S. A.
and
University of Toronto Press, Toronto, Canada

1 9 6 9

Printed by The Anthoensen Press, Portland, Maine, U. S. A.

Contents

Preface

THE *longevity of Joseph F. W. DesBarres (1721-1824) is in itself remarkable for an eighteenth-century figure. His public careers spanned three countries and six decades. Unfortunately we know very little about him as a private person, only strong hints here and there that he was pigheaded, irascible, litigious, and the father of a brood of children who took on many of these same qualities. Time and again in telling the story of his life I have cried out for some flesh to put on the bones of his public actions, but usually long searches have turned up nothing more concrete than a wisp of additional information. Under these provocations it has been tempting on occasion to resort to the myth making which has surrounded DesBarres' name in the region where he is best known, the Maritime provinces of Canada. But I have resisted by reminding myself that this is the work of a historian not a novelist.*

To many of his contemporaries DesBarres was merely a damn nuisance with a prodigious penchant for pestering government officials for more money. This irritating habit could, of course, only spring from an unquenchable optimism which, during the years when he was a British colonial governor (1784-1787 and 1804-1812), became transformed into large claims concerning the future of the colonies for which he was responsible. Few recognized in the foreign-born servant of the British Crown the genius which led him to produce in his collection of charts, The Atlantic Neptune, *a magnificent contribution to hydrography and a classic of the minor arts. One can only wish that he had been free to devote himself entirely to the chart making he did so superbly, but his own character and ambitions allied to the exigencies of the time did not permit it. As a result, DesBarres spent years of his life warming seats in the anterooms of Whitehall and drawing up long, earnest, and sometimes ill-tempered statements of his services complete with extremely detailed financial accounts to prove how much the British government owed him! When he was actually doing his surveying (1763-1773) he had a sideline in land specula-*

tion, an activity common to military officers in his day. Turning his training to good advantage he managed to become one of the largest landowners in the Maritimes and also brought upon himself and his family a multitude of legal problems.

The story of DesBarres, therefore, does not fit neatly into any of the pigeonholes of history. It crosses geographical boundaries and the professional limits of our more specialized age. It involves a number of technical topics, from maritime surveying to eighteenth-century land laws, but I have sought to present these in a manner intelligible to the layman by bearing vividly in mind my own plight when I first tackled them. I have also pared down my words so that the essence of DesBarres is presented unhampered by repetitious details of such matters as his numerous lawsuits. Where a reader wishes to pursue a particular point further, may I be permitted to refer him to the Yale University dissertation which formed the first draft of this work; it is available on microfilm. The absence of charts in a work which talks about them at length may cause some surprise. It was found that reproduction on a scale suitable for their inclusion involved reduction to the point where neither their content nor quality would be appreciated. Fortunately there are copies of the Atlantic Neptune in various depositories in the United States, Canada, and Great Britain, and quite recently a modern facsimile edition has been produced. Full references will be found in the Bibliographical Essay under "Maps and Charts."

Over several years and during much travel and correspondence I have incurred a great number of debts in many parts of the world. It is now pleasant to acknowledge them publicly. On cartographical and hydrographical problems I was greatly aided by the suggestions of J. C. Beaglehole, W. C. Crump, Walter B. Greenwood, Theodore Layng, Walter W. Ristow, R. A. Skelton, Eva G. R. Taylor, Alexander O. Vietor, D. W. Waters, T. B. Webb, and Robert L. Williams. Andrew C. Clark, John V. Duncanson, and the late Daniel C. Harvey aided me in finding my way through the interesting thickets of Maritimes history. The way of the historian is always lightened by the pioneering labors of archivists, librarians, and curators. I should like to thank those at the following institutions: American Geographical Society, New York City; Dalhousie University Library, Halifax, N. S.; James McConnell

Preface

Memorial Library, Sydney, N. S.; Municipal Archives, New York City; Museum of the City of New York; Mystic Marine Museum, Mystic, Conn.; New Brunswick Museum, Saint John, N. B.; New York Genealogical and Biographical Society; New-York Historical Society; New York Public Library, Map, Manuscript, and Rare Book Divisions; New York State Historical Association; New York State Library; Public Archives of Nova Scotia, Halifax; Public Archives of Prince Edward Island, Charlottetown; Xavier Junior College, Sydney, N. S. A special debt is owed W. Kaye Lamb and his staff at the hospitable Public Archives of Canada. I should also like to thank Douglas Waugh for drawing the much needed map.

Yale University awarded me the Brinton Fellowship for the period in which much of the research for this book was completed. I am proud to have had that honor. At Yale also, Robin Winks helped me first to meet DesBarres and then encouraged me to persevere when I despaired of explaining his careers. Archibald Foord corrected my stylistic infelicities with gentleness and charm. At the Peabody Museum, Ernest S. Dodge was more than generous in providing technical advice and seeing the manuscript through the press. But the book might not have appeared at all had it not been for the deep interest and warm support of Augustus P. Loring. I cannot adequately express my gratitude for his help. To all who clarified a disputed point or suggested an avenue down which I might track my elusive subject, I tender my heartiest thanks.

Unlike DesBarres I owe a great deal to the institution of matrimony. Although I came to know the chartmaker a little before I set my own course on the sea of marriage, I could have asked for no finer shipmate than my wife, Ursula. That the good ship DesBarres finally comes home to port owes much to her patient navigation, without benefit of any Neptune! *For errors on the course I alone remain responsible.*

Staten Island in New York Harbor
Dominion Day, 1968

UNCOMMON OBDURATE:
THE SEVERAL PUBLIC CAREERS
OF J. F. W. DesBARRES

CHAPTER I

Man of Many Parts

THE Huguenot family of DesBarres had its roots in the county of Montbéliard in southeastern France. At the revocation of the Edict of Nantes in 1685, and the termination thereby of the limited toleration granted to the Protestant group, Jean Vallet des Barres, although a councilor of the province, had to flee to Basle, Switzerland. Some believe that it was there that his grandson Joseph Frederic Vallet was born in 1721. Others have made a claim for Paris, which is a distinct possibility. Still others have spoken of him as a native-born Englishman, but there is no doubt at all that he was not.[1] The question of birthplace is only one of a number of factual pieces in the jigsaw of DesBarres' life about which there cannot, at least at this time, be complete certainty. Fortunately we do have clear evidence on a matter of far greater importance in the shaping of his future greatness. DesBarres was definitely educated at Basle and was lucky enough to have as his teachers members of the Bernouilli family, one of the most distinguished names in the history of Mathematics. DesBarres' mentors were John (1667-1748) and one of his sons, Daniel (1700-1782). Could anyone have foreseen in the boy the remarkable hydrographer he became, they could hardly have found on the European horizon a more brilliant or pertinent education.

1. Concerning the date of DesBarres' birth see John C. Webster, *The Life of Joseph Frederick Wallet DesBarres* (privately printed, Shediac, N. B., 1933), pp. 8-9 and "Joseph Frederick Wallet DesBarres and The Atlantic Neptune," *Transactions*, Royal Society of Canada, 3d Series, XXI (1927), Sec. 2, pp. 21-22. Webster also declared that DesBarres was born in Switzerland, on the basis of a statement by DesBarres made in a letter to Lord Sydney, dated October 15, 1792. Although Webster's conclusion was a sensible one, it contradicted another statement by DesBarres made in the anonymously published *Letters to Lord * * * * on a Caveat against Emigration to America* (London, 1804) that he was not a native of Switzerland. James S. Macdonald and Charles W. Vernon both stated that DesBarres was born in Paris. See *Montreal Gazette*, November 22, 1913, p. 15, and *Halifax Morning Chronicle*, January 1, 1914, p. 14. Macdonald believed DesBarres' father was Joseph Frederic DesBarres of Geneva, who died in 1727. Webster declared the father to be Joseph Leonard DesBarres. Part of the confusion stems from the paucity of vital statistics, but part may also be blamed on DesBarres who does not seem to have wished his antecedents known. Since he began his military career in the Seven Years War against France and spent all his adult life in the service of the British Crown his attitude, if he was indeed born in Paris, is entirely understandable!

The Bernouillis were in the forefront of the exciting mathematical advances which occurred in the last quarter of the seventeenth century and the first quarter of the eighteenth. John became professor of mathematics at Basle in 1705 and Daniel, who had been professor of mathematics at St. Petersburg when he was only twenty-five, returned as a professor of anatomy and botany in 1733. In keeping with his mathematical bent he was later given a chair in physics. His achievements gave him a claim to the elusive title of one of the founders of mathematical physics. From such masters DesBarres received an exceptional training in theoretical as well as applied mathematics at a time in the intellectual history of Europe when men were daring to apply Reason with both vigor and imagination. Some went too far, and in their attempt to solve Mankind's eternal questions by something very akin to an universal calculus were bound to fail. But with what glory! The air of discovery made possible new answers and produced radical changes in men's modes of thought. In the endeavor to find the mathematical laws of nature, which had been pushed forward by the towering minds of Descartes, Galileo, Newton, and Leibnitz, distinctions between pure mathematics, applied mathematics, and science became blurred and men like Adrien Legendre, Pierre Laplace or the Bernouillis easily crossed the previously accepted lines of demarcation.

In his own work DesBarres continued this process of integration. He left Switzerland and became a cadet at the Royal Military Academy at Woolwich, near London some time in 1752 or 1753. This date and a number of other details in his early career are difficult to pin down, but the broad contours are clear and thanks to the Army's penchant for precision there is a record of his entering military service with a commission in the Royal American Regiment on February 23, 1756.[2] The usual length of time for someone at Woolwich was three or four years. Although one might think that in view of his previous training DesBarres' course might have been shortened, there is no evidence of this and, considering the problems involved in transferring

2. Lewis W. G. Butler, *The Annals of the King's Royal Rifle Corps* (5 vols.; London, 1913), I, Appendix VI, p. 346, hereafter cited as Butler, *Rifle Corps*. Statement of the service of Major DesBarres, May 1, 1784, DesBarres Papers, Series III, p. 78. The Royal American Regiment was also numbered the 62d, but in 1757 it became the 60th Regiment. It continued to be known as the Royal American and remained in America until 1773. In 1824, the 60th became The Duke of York's Own Rifle Corps and then, in 1830, The King's Royal Rifle Corps.

college "credits" across international boundaries even today, it seems unlikely in the haughty English educational system of the eighteenth century.

The Academy had been established in 1741 under a royal warrant which declared that its purpose was to give instruction in the branches of mathematics necessary for men who would serve in the Artillery or as Engineers.[3] There was room available at Woolwich Warren, where the Royal Artillery had its headquarters, and until 1744 the cadets simultaneously received training at the Academy and were members of the regimental companies. In that year a separate unit "The Company of Gentlemen Cadets" was formed. Its members lodged "at the most creditable houses in and near Woolwich" until accommodations were built for them in 1752. Once the barracks were established an officer was detailed to keep an eye on the cadets during lectures, mealtimes, and parades and run a bed check to see that they were in by their curfew hour. As always the authorities and the young men did not see eye to eye and in practice the cadets had considerable independence in both personal and academic matters.

DesBarres, an older student and a foreigner, could not have felt "one of the gang" and probably did not receive very much intellectual stimulation to offset his loneliness. The training at Woolwich seems to have been of a high order and covered a wide range of mathematics, but little could have been new to a former pupil of the Bernouillis. Nor could he benefit greatly from the teaching of French and drawing; the first was his native language, the second a part of his education in Switzerland. What DesBarres did gain was experience in speaking and writing English and some training in the application of mathematical principles to military problems. His classes in fortification, land drainage, surveying, and gunnery offered him newer material than those in geometry, algebra, trigonometry, and conic sections and represented the Army's contribution toward turning a mathematician into an engineer.

During this period the Academy was still groping toward an effective organization. There were no regulations regarding age of entry

3. Brigadier Oliver F. G. Hogg, *The Royal Arsenal* (2 vols.; London, 1963), I, 345-47, hereafter cited as Hogg, *Royal Arsenal*, has made a case for the founding of the Academy in 1720. It is doubtful, however, if regular instruction took place or that the institution was functioning before 1741. The author agrees with Sir John Smyth, *Sandhurst* (London, 1961), p. 28, that "the 1721 warrant was never really implemented."

and no promise of appointment on "passing out." If he survived the sordid living conditions and attended some of the classes, the cadet was tested by a few questions before a Board of Officers. No proper final examination was given and after graduation only one of the two branches of the army for which the Academy was supposed to train officers was really open. Until the formation of the Corps of Engineers in 1759 warrant officers sufficed.[4] Vacancies in the Royal Artillery (or later in the Royal Engineers) rarely occurred when needed, and many a cadet became tired of waiting and joined the East India Company or one of the regiments of the line. So, from the day of entry to the day of departure, he was affected by the Academy's shortcomings.

Although DesBarres was one of those unable to find a place in the Royal Artillery Regiment, the unit he did join is one of special interest. The Royal American Regiment was created on the basis of the idea of James Prevost, a Swiss mercenary, who originally badgered the British government to raise troops for overseas service by using deserters from the scores of German princely armies. The scheme was quickly extended to include German and Swiss settlers in the colonies themselves. After the sharp defeat of Braddock at Fort Duquesne in July 1755, the manpower needs of the American front were more clearly perceived at home. An act was passed in February 1756 legalizing what Prevost had been up to for many months, namely recruitment in Europe in defiance of the legal obstacles in the Act of Settlement (1701) prohibiting foreign officers from holding British commissions.[5]

American events and European enterprise had combined to effect an important change in British army policy.[6] The novelty of the recruitment and the character of the leaders it obtained were to lead to interesting advances in military tactics. Even before the act was through Parliament Viscount Barrington, the Secretary at War, was

4. Even the custom of commissioning cadets first in the Artillery and then in the Engineers prevailed until 1761. After 1761, cadets were commissioned directly to the Corps of Engineers. See Hogg, *Royal Arsenal*, I, 355.

5. Great Britain, *Statutes at Large*, 29 Geo. II, c. 5. Note that the commissions applied only to service in North America.

6. Pitt utilized the opportunity to attack the military plans of the Newcastle administration. In this opposition he was joined by a number of the colonial agents, notably Bollan of Massachusetts. See Stanley McC. Pargellis, *Lord Loudoun in North America* ("Yale Historical Publications, Studies," VII, New Haven, 1933), 63, hereafter cited as Pargellis, *Lord Loudoun*.

giving instructions that the regiment's clothing should be suitable for brush warfare. Henry Bouquet, its first lieutenant colonel, conceived and perfected new ways of fighting the Indians and eventually came to be regarded as one of the finest tacticians in a century which produced more than its share of them. The Royal Americans also paid careful attention to weapons, horses, encampment, and line of march.[7] In executing Bouquet's design of bringing a little of the flexibility of the French into a British army patterned on the Prussian model, they acquired some of the traits of the American frontier fighter to blend in with their more traditional training.

DesBarres was one of the first to be commissioned in the new regiment. Many of its officers had several years of European service and quite a few (Bouquet, Frederick Haldimand, and both James and Augustine Prevost for example), were of Swiss birth yet, rather surprisingly in view of the original intention, a larger number were British. DesBarres sailed for America in the spring of 1756 as an engineer attached to the regiment. But his first job had little to do with his technical skills. With the other recently arrived officers he was told to raise recruits and given the ticklish assignment of doing so in Quaker Pennsylvania. The men he obtained there and in Maryland were formed into a corps of field artillery which he commanded until a battalion of the Royal Artillery Regiment came out from England.

Since there is no totally reliable picture of the depositions of the various battalions between 1756 and 1758 the movements of Des Barres, a specialized officer, are even less clear.[8] In 1757 he was at Schenectady, New York and took part in an attack on the Indians, but later in the year he sailed to Louisbourg, Cape Breton Island with the second and third battalions. There he was able to concentrate on engineering problems. Even more important for his later career, French documents and plans came into his possession after the British had captured the fortress. During the winter of 1758 he began work which by the next year had produced a large scale chart of the St. Lawrence. Together with others, such as the ones made by young James Cook, it was used when Wolfe moved up the river to Quebec City. The taking

7. Bouquet's ideas may be most conveniently found in Butler, *Rifle Corps*, I, 3-4, 26, 159-67, Appendix IV, pp. 330-34.

8. The movements of the battalions are narrated in Butler, *Rifle Corps*, I, 28-30, 33-43, and Pargellis, *Lord Loudoun*, pp. 178, 198-211.

of the French capital then gave DesBarres a chance to work on surveys of the city and the surrounding area. After Montreal fell to the British in 1760, he was posted back to Halifax to work under Colonel John Bastide in drawing up plans and estimates for its defences and dockyard.[9]

Before the Seven Years War was over there came still another opportunity to broaden his knowledge and improve his hydrographic techniques. In 1762, when the victor in North America was for all practical purposes decided, a British expedition under Colonel William Amherst was sent to Newfoundland to recapture Saint John's. DesBarres went along as both engineer and quartermaster general. Once the mission had achieved its objective, he had the chance to survey many of the island's principal harbors. In six years of military service he had been given invaluable experience as an engineer and map maker as well as brief contact with the life of a regular army officer. All his wide-ranging activities were borne in mind when Jeffrey Amherst, the colonel's brother and commander in chief since 1758, summoned DesBarres to New York in 1763. The general's intention seems to have been to have DesBarres compile reports on various fortifications in America but nothing came from this harmless bit of nepotism. Amherst was recalled before a new assignment for DesBarres could be made and what finally developed was quite different. The army engineer came to the attention of a senior naval officer, Captain Richard Spry, and very soon he found himself back in the Maritime provinces of Canada as a seconded servant of the Admiralty. DesBarres' career and future became bound up with that region and his next ten years of work ultimately gave him fame as a chart maker such as had never seemed likely to befall him as a soldier.

9. See Report on Halifax fortifications, 1761, in Records of the Nova Scotia Command, Vol. 1425, Public Archives of Canada, Ottawa, hereafter PAC.

CHAPTER II

To the Sea in Ships

DESBARRES and the small number of other hydrographers in his generation were fortunate beneficiaries of a "scientific revolution" spanning the period 1660-1760. He was by temperament more of a practical than a theoretical scientist and therefore lucky that his times did not demand that he be a pioneer. Hydrography was no different from any other area of science when it came to rapid and radical advance. The 1730's provide some good examples. Almost simultaneously John Hadley in England and Thomas Godfrey in America developed the octant or reflecting quadrant.[1] In 1734 the restless mind of Hadley saw further possibilities. He fixed a spirit level to his instrument and thereby allowed a meridian altitude to be taken at sea even when the horizon was not visible.[2] The first of John Harrison's many chronometers also appeared in this decade and eventually when its value began to be realized it was perceived that its use in conjunction with the octant and the almanac enabled a navigator to compute latitude and longitude every day and to calculate the position of a ship independently of what he reached on the basis of "dead reckoning." With these and other developments the essential tools of an accurate hydrography were being created and the way was open for the precise practice of scientific principles.[3]

It was about time! To an amazing extent man's knowledge of the seas had rested upon the vision of certain renowned explorers and the raw courage of countless maritime folk. There was considerable reliance on the results of Ancient science right through to the sixteenth century, but continued dependence on the work of the Mediterranean cultures was unacceptable once the North European nations had not

1. See Hadley's account in *Philosophical Transactions*, Royal Society of London, XXXVII (1731), 147-57 and a shortened version in Charles Hulton, George Shaw, and Richard Pearson (eds.), *The Philosophical Transactions, Abridged* (18 vols.; London, 1809), VII, 486-94.

2. *Philosophical Transactions*, Royal Society of London, XXXVIII (1733), 167-72. Scrutiny of the *Transactions* for the period 1730-1770 makes immediately clear the intense interest in the development of better navigational and astronomical instruments.

3. In addition to the advances indicated in the text, the appearance of the first edition of the *Nautical Almanac* in 1766, for use in the following year, is worthy of note.

only crossed the Atlantic but established colonies on the other side. A second impetus came by 1750 or so when it was more generally recognized that though mapping of land areas was not as detailed or as accurate as it should be, it was superior to what was available for the surrounding waters. In this respect Britain was hardly better off than its Continental rivals. When Greenvile Collins, Charles II's Hydrographer in Ordinary, undertook a coastal survey of Great Britain in 1682 he was forced to report that the bulk of the existing charts had been made by the Dutch, so lately the enemy in the English Channel. It was only a minor consolation that they were full of mistakes! Collins put his finger on the amateur character of the trade, an aspect which continued into DesBarres' day, when he asked that "those persons who make and sell sea-charts and maps . . . not [be] allowed to alter them upon the single report of mariners, but with your approbation; by which means our sea-charts would be correct, and the common scandal of their badness removed."[4]

English hydrography can be traced back as far as Antony Ashley's *Mariner's Mirror* (1588) but this was little more than a republication of Lucas Waghenaer's *Spiegel der Zeevaert*. The first truly native achievement was Collins' *Coasting Pilot* (1693) which was based on a rather crude method of marine chart making known as the "running survey." As a result the charts showed latitude only occasionally and longitude markings were entirely absent. Until the work of DesBarres in American and his contemporary Murdoch Mackenzie the Elder (d. 1797) in British waters, the art was still at a pretty primitive stage. The truth of this is attested to by the very large amount (£10,000) offered by the British government in 1713 to anyone who could fix longitude to one degree, or sixty geographical miles. Greater accuracy was to be further rewarded, correctness to forty miles by £15,000 and to thirty miles by £20,000. Between 1730 and 1765 John Harrison (1693-1776), an untutored but brilliant horologist, responded to the challenge by devising a series of chronometers to correct errors in reckoning ship's courses. For his efforts he received recognition, praise, the Royal Society's Copley Medal, and a lengthy taste of how a parsimonious Parliament could promise much and give little. Harrison never did get his due under the Board of Longitude's

4. Greenvile Collins, *Great Britain's Coasting Pilot* (London, 1776 edition), Preface.

[10]

offer and it took a host of petitions, a special law, a demonstration before the Astronomer Royal, Nevil Maskelyne, and the lapse of forty years before he obtained a sizable part of the prize money. Later in the century, DesBarres was to suffer in a similar way.

Slowly the British were equipping themselves to challenge the supremacy of the French in map and chart making. For a hundred years or more the rival giants had fought each other in a series of wars, with an inevitable impetus to arts so closely linked to military and political power. As the century progressed the British gradually gained ground, in both cartography and conquest. Their victory in the Seven Years War struck a shattering blow at the French empire in North America and created new problems for themselves. Two of these, the governing of Canada and the establishing of a systematic survey of all American possessions, were especially relevant to DesBarres' career. For the cartographical work the colonies were divided into a Northern and Southern district, each with its surveyor general. In the North he was Samuel Holland, in the South William De-Brahm. Holland, born near Nijmegen about 1728, was an amiable man who after mathematical training enlisted in the Dutch Army before transferring to the British. His early career resembles that of DesBarres. He was an officer in the Royal American Regiment and served in New York in military, engineering, and cartographic capacities. In 1758 both were engineer officers under Wolfe and later said they were present at his death.[5] Both were assisted by James Cook and in a sense helped to train him as a hydrographer, and each was employed in strengthening the fortifications at Quebec after its capture. Then in 1761 Holland was busy making surveys of the settled parts of the province and in the following year, when DesBarres was serving in the expedition to recapture Newfoundland, he returned to England where he showed his plans to the Board of Trade. DeBrahm (1717-c. 1799), another Dutch military engineer, played an im-

5. The number of men who have claimed that they were there when Wolfe died has led one scholar to exclaim that it is a wonder that anyone was left to fight the French! It seems proven that, after the capture of Louisbourg, Holland gave instruction in the techniques of surveying to the young James Cook. See Willis Chipman, "The Life and Times of Major Samuel Holland," *Papers and Records*, Ontario Hist. Soc., XXI (1924), 18-20, quoting from a manuscript printed by H. Scadding. The full reference for Scadding's note is *Canadian Magazine*, VI (October 1895), 522-24. On his plan of Quebec and its environs (1759) DesBarres noted the assistance of Cook, especially in the task of making soundings.

portant role in the early days of Georgia's history, although even more of his mapping work concerned the Florida coastline, the treacherous Keys, and some of the inland areas. The Board of Trade's arrangement for surveying the American colonies left no place for DesBarres, except perhaps as Holland's assistant. Too proud to have accepted this, even if it had been offered to him, he made his own preparations. During the next decade, that is almost to the eve of the American Revolution, while Holland surveyed the eastern parts of North America under the orders of the Lords of Trade DesBarres concentrated his energies on the nearby coasts under the direction of the Lords of the Admiralty.

The two men did not carry out joint surveys and corresponded only to a minimal extent, but their results were finally brought together. The *Atlantic Neptune*, the source of DesBarres' fame as a hydrographer and the pinnacle of his achievements, was based quite as much on the work of the Dutchman, but the compilation, editing and, most important of all, the adaptation of the existing materials for use by the British navy during the War of Independence was done entirely by DesBarres and his assistants. At no time did he present the total contents of the *Neptune* as his own. In a huge mass of supplicatory letters, repetitive memoranda, and tangled accounting statements in connection with his hydrographic labors there is no instance of his claiming credit for the work of others. It should also be remembered that these activities took place before the establishment of the Admiralty's Hydrographic Office in 1795 and its Chart Committee in 1807, the official bodies created as supervisors for British chart making. When DesBarres was preparing his work for publication amateur hydrographers, military engineers, and private publishers were all vying with one another. Copyright laws frequently were thrown overboard in a flurry of national and international plagiarism. Under these conditions, DesBarres' acknowledgments are all the more estimable.

Between 1764 and 1766 Holland surveyed Saint John's Island (renamed Prince Edward Island in 1799) and Cape Breton Island, ironically the two colonies where DesBarres was later to be governor. In the next four years Holland and his assistants also surveyed and mapped portions of the lower St. Lawrence River, many of its tributaries, and the upper St. Lawrence from Montreal to Oswegatchie, a fort near the present Ogdensburg, New York. Then, headquartered at Kittery near Portsmouth, New Hampshire, he dealt with eastern New England. He began work by continuing a survey commenced by DesBarres, and eventually the work of the two surveyors connected up, on the west at the Saint John River, on the east at the Gut of Canso. Before leaving North America Holland may have pushed his surveys as far south as Cape Cod, concentrating less than DesBarres did on the strictly hydrographic aspects. Neither man has told us as much as we would like to know about the methods used, but the quality of the charts in the *Neptune*, especially those we can attribute totally to DesBarres, testify to a superb craftsmanship. In general, the hydrographers of the eighteenth century did not say a great deal as to how they went about their tasks. Procedures were still being handed down on a personal basis and although there were several manuals for land surveying no complementary literature for the chart maker had yet been written. Fortunately a letter from the first years of DesBarres' survey has survived. It proves that he had progressed well beyond the techniques of Collins' generation, and was fully applying the mathematical and instrumental developments of the intervening years. In reporting to his superior, Alexander, Lord Colville on the work of the previous summer he indicated both his basic method and an interesting variation. So rare are such insights that it is here reproduced in detail:[6]

I measured a base of 350 fathoms along a plane on the western side of Exeter Harbour, and from its extreemities, having, with a theodolite, taken the angles of visual rays to objects placed on the opposite shore, which being calculated trigonometrically and protracted in their proper bearings on paper fixed upon a plain table, I then repeated, with the plain table, the same operations over again, and intersected the same objects from the same extreemities of the base line, by which and other intersections, or series of triangles, I had the distance between an object placed on Point Bulkeley and another on Newton Head; from whence, by further intersections performed in the same manner, I determined the true emplacement of Winter's, Roger's and Barron's Islands, and of all the ledges; thence, repeating the former operations from all these islands. I found all the angles, and distances to agree with what I had layd down, from the above mentioned observations, before. From points as were most commodi-

6. DesBarres to Colville, May 1765, Adm. Sec. In Letters (Adm. 1-482) Originals at Public Record Office, London, microfilm copies at Library of Congress, Washington, D. C. See also G. N. D. Evans, "Hydrography: A Note on Eighteenth Century Methods," *Mariner's Mirror*, LII (1966), 247-50.

ously situated on those islands, and head lands, I observed the distant head lands, bays, islands, points, and other remarkable objects, as far as they could be distinguished. Next I went along shore, and reexamined the accuracy of every intersected object, delineated the true shape of every head land, island, point, bay, rock above water, etc and every winding and irregularity of the coast; and, with boats sent around the shoals, rocks and breakers, determined from observations on shore, their position and extent, as perfectly as I could. When the map of any part of the coast was compleated in this manner, I provided immediately each craft with copys of it: The sloop was employed in beating off and on, upon the coast, to the distance of ten and twelve miles in the offing, laying down the soundings in their proper bearings and distance, remarking every where the quality of the bottom. The shallop was, in the meantime, kept busy in sounding, and remarking around the headlands, islands, and rocks in the offing; and the boats within the indraught, upwards, to the heads of bays, har:^{rs} etc.

The irregular and broken character of the coastline and the thickly wooded nature of the terrain convinced DesBarres that he would have difficulty in finding convenient places of the requisite levelness and length. He therefore supplemented his first techniques with the following, more experimental one:

I soaked a dipsey line in salt water, till it was fully imbibed, and then stretched and rubbed it tought, and with an iron chain, measured 100 fathoms of it, with marks at every 10 fathoms. Just before the change of the tide, on a calm day, I fixed the one end of this 100 fathom line to a station on Point Bulkeley and, with the other end, rowed right out for another station on Newton Head; (whose distance I already knew) when I got the line tought, I made its end fast to the grapnell, and let it run to the ground; After this, I caused another boat to take the first end (which was fixed to the station on shore) and hawl in the whole line till it came to be perpendicular with the grapnell let down by the first boat and thence to proceed rowing out again for the said station on Newton Head, till the line got to be tought, made fast to the grapnell, and let down as before; And so continued: By which measurement, I found the distance to be 510 fathoms; longer by 5 feet than I had found it by intersections. This same method I repeated in the mensuration of a line from the same station on Point Bulkeley to an object on Roger's Island, and found 1586 fathoms to be the distance; longer, by 19 feet than I had found it to be, by the method of triangles. Many subsequent tryalls and examinations of this new method have convinced me how surprisingly it coincides with mensurations performed, by the means of an iron chain, on shore, and, from these considerations and other cogent reasons, I have been induced to apply it very advantageously during the course of my survey.

The first method DesBarres described is the triangulation used by the best marine surveyors of the time. Murdoch Mackenzie spoke of three major ways of doing a survey. The first was the "running survey," used by Collins. The second was scathingly condemned as chart making on the basis of "verbal Information, copied journals, or superficial sketches of sailors casually passing along the coast." The third, applied by Mackenzie himself, was very similar to the first method described in DesBarres' report.

If it had been more rhythmic, accuracy, more accuracy, and still more accuracy could have been the shanty for such men as Mackenzie and DesBarres. Surveying the coastline was only the beginning of their task. Results had to be put on paper and then compared once again with the actual landmarks, especially with regard to bearings. The variations in the lie of the land, the exact nature and size of shoals and rocks, the depth and quality of the bottom at as many points as possible, the best entry and exit channels, the speed and regularity of the tides, all these were essential pieces of information for the mariner. The majority of contemporary charts were of least value where most needed. General routes from one coast to another were clearly depicted but inshore waters were very poorly mapped. Either the charts were on too small a scale or, when the size was satisfactory, vital details were omitted. Mackenzie said bluntly that "sailors dare not rely on them in times of danger and difficulty."

The benefits to be derived from detailed surveys of American coastal waters were less obvious to the British government than were land surveys offering information on which to base estimates of the economic potential of the colonial possessions. Captain Richard Spry and then Colville, who succeeded him as commodore and naval commander in chief in North America, had to work hard to persuade even the Admiralty that accurate charts were necessary. One of their principal arguments was the abundance of fine harbors, for example in Nova Scotia. Prevailing attitudes as well as the difficulties involved are reflected in the fact that DesBarres only got the job of making the surveys after more senior men had turned it down.[7] Here, as so often is the case, technicians were well ahead of their governments in ap-

7. The problems were clearly indicated in John Green, *Remarks, in Support of the New Chart of North and South America* (1753). Copies, with the chart, exist in Franklin Collection, the Map Room, and Western Americana Collection, Yale University Library.

preciating possibilities and projecting rewards. Some Frenchmen were dissatisfied with the available charts even at the time of their country's obvious superiority. The Marquis de Chabert, to take a prominent example, pointed out that current charts were so bad that in some cases they showed differences of nine degrees of longitude for the same position.[8] Yet the French government's department of plans and charts had been well directed and its employees were frequently at the top of their profession. In the Gulf of St. Lawrence Jacques Nicolas Bellin had produced fine charts but English criticism of them, even after making all necessary allowances for chauvinism, revealed the room for improvement.

DesBarres' work filled this need, and showed he could execute the surveying, draw with magnificent artistry, and supervise excellent engraving. One of the reasons for England lagging behind the French was that the map-making trade, lacking artists, had employed engravers "whose skill consists in supplying the print-sellers with their productions in the most expeditious manner, and at the lowest rates." In DesBarres the engraver and the artist, the technical and the esthetic, were beautifully combined. The charts could not be without blemish but no rival was able to say of them, as one did of Bellin, that he "had committed very gross mistakes, partly by relying on certain observations of longitude, which at best were very doubtful and wanted to be verify'd; partly by depending on erroneous charts, made by former geographers, without giving them a due examination; and partly, by either rejecting the accurate journals of eminent navigators, or else unreasonably straining them, in favour of his own ideas, and the doubtful observations before-mentioned."[9]

It was well that DesBarres placed no great reliance on the extant material; only a few of the maps available to him had even the latitudes marked. Charles Morris, Sr., had made fairly accurate maps of Nova Scotia in 1748-1749, with indications of soundings, tides, and currents, yet he had misplaced Port Royal by eighteen minutes. Although Champlain had given an excellent description of Penobscot Bay in 1604 his fellow countryman Bellin, more than a century later,

8. Joseph Bernard, Marquis de Chabert de Cogolin, *Voyage fait par Ordre du Roi en 1750 et 1751, dans L'Amérique Septentrionale* (Paris, 1753), p. 2.

9. John Green, *Remarks, in Support of the New Chart* (London, 1753), p. 4.

had apparently ignored it. The English map publisher Thomas Jefferys cogently observed in 1755 that "the generality of mariners seem to know of no quality in observing latitudes, farther than to find the place where they are bound to; and when they come in sight of land, lay the quadrant aside, as an instrument no longer of use, and sail by direction of the coast." The geographer was often too broad in his observations, the mariner too inaccurate, regarding "an error of 8 or 10 minutes but a trifle."[10] DesBarres avoided most of the faults of both, while combining their virtues.

Nova Scotian waters were an obvious place to start. The province had been officially in English hands since 1713 and after the Treaty of Aix-la-Chapelle in 1748 thousands of pounds had been spent in building a fortress for British military and naval operations in North America. DesBarres had come to know the region well through service there, in the Gulf, and in Newfoundland. To the navy it was of special concern because Halifax also offered one of the finest harbors on the Atlantic seaboard, ice free in winter, in every season excellent for controlling the approaches to Canada and the New England colonies and within striking distance of the West Indian possessions. Although DesBarres would never have admitted it and the Admiralty may not have cared a great deal, a further advantage was that his work complemented that of Holland on the land.

He seems to have had no clearly recognized staff. From time to time naval officers sought to work with him or he recruited them, and a temporary transfer was arranged. By removing themselves from beneath their commodore's eyes and doing specialized work, these young men may well have lessened their chances of reaching the very highest military levels. Nevertheless, one of his chief assistants, John Knight, ended his career as an admiral. DesBarres, though quite low in rank himself, seems to have adopted a paternal attitude toward his "young gentlemen." He played host, an expense which he later calculated averaged half a guinea a day, although when he tried to claim a rebate from the Admiralty their lordships pointed out that the naval

10. Murdoch Mackenzie, *Orcades; or a Geographic and Hydrographic Survey of the Orkney and Lewis Islands in Eight Maps* (London, 1776), Preface. For an even more devastating analysis of the inaccuracies of existing maps and charts of the area surveyed by DesBarres, see *Explanation for the New Map of Nova Scotia and Cape Breton with the Adjacent Parts of New England and Canada* (printed for Thomas Jefferys, London, 1755).

officers had been allowed their wages and victuals.[11] But if one considers the commissariat of the time it is doubtful that men detached to somewhat remote places on survey work actually received more than a portion of their supplies. DesBarres took advantage of his knowledge of French to hire several Acadians but this decision, excellent as it was in view of their familiarity with both the country and the coastline, added to his financial embarrassments. He asked Captain Samuel Hood, Colville's successor as commodore, to seek Admiralty permission for payment of their wages through Halifax but, with his customary combination of enthusiasm for the task and impatience with the torpidity of bureaucrats, went ahead and employed the Acadians before such consent arrived.

Small open boats known as shallops were used for taking the inshore soundings. In 1770 DesBarres had a larger vessel, the *Diligent*, acting as stores-ship during the actual surveying. But ships, as well as staff, were neither easy to find nor to replace, although on those rocky, treacherous shores they had a high mortality rate. DesBarres was continuously requesting that more vessels be put at his disposal. During the summer, if he could attract the Acadians away from their harvesting, he might have a fairly large number of men engaged in surveying. During the winter, the much smaller group of navy men who were either trained or apprentice assistants clustered around DesBarres in his home, Castle Frederick near Falmouth, Nova Scotia. Howling winds and icy sleet pummeled the wooden walls and tore through the men when they ventured outside. Within, by the glow of candles and lamps and under the eagle eye of their leader, the men toiled to translate the summer's work into intricate charts with the highest possible accuracy. The lieutenant, for such was his army rank, tried to introduce a note of elegance into the long days and longer nights by keeping a good table and adding an artistic flourish or two to the charts as they were produced. He was a dedicated worker but, perhaps as a consequence, reckless in his disregard of official procedures. He laid down "as a rule of conduct to avail myself of the ability of every person I met who could assist me in carrying on the surveys." Paying them out of

11. DesBarres to Philip Stephens, November 13, 1769, DesBarres Papers, Series V, p. 52. Later, the decision was reversed and the allowance was given to DesBarres, Lords of the Admiralty to Committee of the Privy Council, October 21, 1782, DesBarres Papers, Series III, p. 58.

his own pocket, he was slowly forming a group which was partially beholden to him for food and shelter and bound to him by interest in an art where he was proving himself a master. After ten years they had done the work which was turned into the first part of the *Neptune* and DesBarres, who was always a little too proud and a little too jealous, nevertheless had a point when he later asked, a little rhetorically, "who would even in speculation compare the utility of making the seas known and safe for British navigation to that of surveying interior wood land and townships."

In the eyes of bureaucrats a rash and impatient man, in his work he was extremely painstaking. Two years were spent in surveying the Isle of Sable alone. Economically the island was worthless, but it lay close to major shipping lanes. At both ends sandbars ran out into the ocean for more than fifteen miles; its coasts had no harbors but plenty of fogs and storms; currents swirled around it in very irregular ways. It had properly earned the reputation of being one of the Atlantic's most populated graveyards.[12] DesBarres was therefore fully justified in charting this dangerous area early on in his work and taking such a long time over it. His amazing eye for detail gathered data about the vegetation, climate, winds, velocity and direction of currents, as well as the usual, basic information on bearings. The resulting charts were probably his tour de force as a marine surveyor, although the difficulties and dangers he overcame in making them were repeated on a lesser scale at many other places.

By November 1769, he was able to send the Admiralty charts of the Isle of Sable, the eastern part of Nova Scotia, Chedabucto Bay, Richmond Isles, and the Gut of Canso, yet he was constantly unhappy with the slow rate of progress. He believed it was due to the insufficient number of men allowed him. In 1764 he had been fairly well content with a sloop, three boats, and a shallop but the Sable survey created additional demands. A small schooner was what was really required but it would have to be manned by British sailors since the owners who had hired out the sloop provided only enough men to sail their own vessel. The senior officer at Halifax had no men to spare but told the

---

12. There have been over 200 known shipwrecks on the coast of the island and the number of unrecorded tragedies is believed to be much higher. On DesBarres' work, in addition to the notably meticulous charts in the *Atlantic Neptune*, see DesBarres to Colville, July 28, 1766. DesBarres Papers, Series V, p. 39.

surveyor to hire any he could find. With great difficulty a number were taken on, some at fifty shillings and some at forty-five shillings per month. DesBarres also appealed to his old supporter Commodore Hood, who ordered twenty-eight sailors to be placed on the supernumerary list of H.M.S. *Romney*. After further petitions he was lent the *Diligent* but the men from the *Romney* were discharged and Des-Barres, who needed time to train and organize men, once more found himself with a labor shortage.

"One of the most remarkable products of human industry that has ever been given to the world through the arts of printing and engraving" and "the most splendid collection of charts, plans and views ever published."[13] These verdicts, by a Frenchman and an American, on the charts DesBarres gathered together as the *Atlantic Neptune* hardly exceed the truth. No description can do full justice to these magnificent volumes any more than words can substitute for seeing a fine painting, but a few general characteristics may be indicated. Indeed, it is essential to speak in general terms because no two *Neptunes* are the same. The copies can be divided into two types; the folio with plates of full size and the narrow folio with the plates folded vertically. There were four editions, appearing in 1777, 1780, 1781, and 1784. At irregular intervals special groups were made up for individual captains when DesBarres or an assistant simply pulled down from the shelves one copy of each chart deemed relevant.

In 1778 he published as a pilot to the first part of the *Neptune* a short piece compiled in large part from the directions which had previously appeared on individual charts and titled *Nautical Remarks and Observations on the Coasts and Harbours of Nova Scotia*. His writing had two characteristics clearly visible in the charts themselves: it was the result of a sharp eye noting every detail of land and sea which could possibly aid a mariner, and it was presented in a consciously artistic fashion. Describing the coast from Canso to Torbay, he remarked that "the shore makes in several white rocky heads and points; here the country is much broken, and near White Head many white stones appear from the offing like sheep in the woods." He easily maintained the reader's

13. See *L'Esprit des Journaux* (Paris, 1784), III, 459-74, translated in Isaac N. P. Stokes, *The Iconography of Manhattan Island* (6 vols.; New York, 1915-28), I, 349, and Obadiah Rich, *Bibliotheca Americana Nova* (2 vols.; London and New York, 1835-44), I, 249.

interest during further general remarks before moving to the second, and much longer, part which consisted of tables of such technical matters as latitude, time of high water, and vertical rise of the tide. For the more important harbors there were additional piloting directions revealing an astounding familiarity with the places in question.[14]

Since no definitive list of plates is available, and the number of variant printings is as many as ten for each plate, no one may claim to have a "complete" *Atlantic Neptune*. The determination of variants is an extremely technical matter which, however, can be briefly summarized. Where a chart has no imprint, identification is made upon the basis of the paper's watermark since even when there are no cartographical differences the type of paper makes clear the priority of issue. There are six different watermarks, with a small number of charts printed on paper having a mixed mark. Other aids in dating an individual chart are plate numbers, shown on only a minority of sheets but useful in determining the order of formation for a bound collection, stipled shoals and settlements, and overall coloring. Catalogues provide an index and allow comparisons as to the completeness of each collection.[15]

Dividing the *Atlantic Neptune* into its component parts presents far fewer problems, if only because DesBarres' own analysis corresponds approximately with a breakdown of the copies we now have. Book I consisted of "impressions of all the charts plates of my surveys of the coast and harbours of Nova Scotia, with a small book of tables of latitudes, longitudes, variations of the magnetic North, tides etc."; Book II contained "charts of the coast and harbours of New England composed, by command of Government, by various surveys, but principally from those taken by Major Holland under the directions of my Lords of Trade and Plantations"; Book III comprised charts of the Gulf of St. Lawrence, and the islands of Cape Breton and St. John; Book IV, the coast of North America south of New York based on several surveys; Book V, "various views of the North American

14: The *Nautical Remarks* is not listed in the *Dictionary of National Biography* articles on DesBarres and copies are rare. The one seen is in the possession of the American Geographical Society, New York.

15. DesBarres published a partial catalogue of the 1781 edition. A copy is in the Harvard College Library. Modern catalogues are listed in the bibliography of this study.

coast."[16] In the final printed versions the views were included with the charts of the corresponding area.

The process of publishing the charts came about in the following way. In 1772 DeBrahm returned to England and both Holland and DesBarres arrived two years later. The two surveyors general went back to North America in 1774 and 1776 respectively and so, by a default similar to that which had led to his hydrographic assignment ten years earlier, the duty of providing charts for the British fleets during the American Revolution fell to DesBarres. In March 1775 the Admiralty approved his publication proposals and list of priorities, and in May he petitioned the Board of Trade for access to the surveys in its offices.[17] Before the year was out he was able to supply Vice Admiral Howe and other officers with some charts. The need to give naval officers precise and up-to-date information on the areas where they were sailing and fighting should have been clear to all, but before he left for America Howe felt it necessary to emphasize it once again to fellow members of the Navy Board. DesBarres was encouraged to hire as many assistants as possible, and at the peak of the operation he crowded two houses with them. Considering the size of the fleet—even this "navy in adversity" had over one hundred capital ships—it was not too many.

The work was not done as quickly as might have been expected. At the end of 1776 the charts in Book I were ready for printing, but the plates for Book II were "very deficient as yet in the soundings and nautical observations." No impressions could yet be taken from the plates for Books III and IV and several of the plates of views (Book V) were in the hands of the engraver awaiting his improvements. The adaptation of Holland's maps, made necessary because they lacked such details as soundings, was in DesBarres' eyes a "most intricate and tedious part of the business." According to him it had been agreed, when both men were engaged on their surveys, that they would exchange maps and Holland proposed "to distinguish in his geographic map what parts he has received of me, and I am likewise to acknowledge those which he may have supplied me should I insert them when

16. DesBarres to Richard Cumberland, received 1778, DesBarres Papers, Series III, p. 97. By internal evidence the letter may be dated as December 20, 1778.

17. Philip Stephens to DesBarres, March 18, 1775, DesBarres Papers, Series V, p. 131. For DesBarres' petition to the Lords of Trade, May 16, see DesBarres Papers, Series III, p. 93.

I come to publish my Sea Charts."[18] Furthermore, Holland would provide him with "astronomic observations and materials (as he names them) by the means of which I am to protract proper sea charts and to improve and compleat same with soundings and necessary observations and remarks, etc peculiarly adapted for the purpose of navigation." For two servants of the same sovereign this was a rather ludicrous arrangement. No one knows who instigated it but in all probability it was the insecure and distrustful DesBarres rather than the more levelheaded and confident Holland. A foreigner working for an England which had not reached such heights of chauvinism since the days of Shakespeare, a poor man struggling to make his way in a profession where advancement depended upon an established system of buying promotion, it should not be too surprising that DesBarres included pettiness and suspicion in a personality which never demonstrated an abundance of the pleasing traits. Even Holland, who much more readily combined tact with talent, had by the end of his life come to nothing higher than surveyor general of Lower Canada.

When the *Neptune* was published, the debt to Holland and others was naturally recognized in a general way. But close examination of the work, its various title pages, the detailed table of contents, and the individual charts shows that proper recognition was indeed given. To take one example, the chart of the southeast coast of the island of St. John carries in its title "surveyed under the direction of the Right Honourable the Lords of Trade and Plantations: By Saml Holland, Esqr. Surv^r Genl of the Northern District of N. America, and Thos Wright, James Grant etc his assistants. Published by Command of Government, by J. F. W. DesBarres." Even by the standards of a later age DesBarres cannot be judged dishonest, and for an era when literary pirating was commonplace the extent of the acknowledgments was extraordinary. It is only fair to DesBarres to add that cartographers and hydrographers recognize that all maps and charts, with only rare exceptions such as the first maps of Antarctica, are largely derivative. A map is made "new" by the addition of information or the correction of hitherto accepted data. By adapting Holland's land surveys for nautical use and particularly by his addition of sound-

18. DesBarres to Hood, August 13, 1770, DesBarres Papers, Series V, p. 56. As one example of DesBarres' claim that the surveys of Holland and DeBrahm were less difficult and less dangerous, see his statement in the Memorial to the Privy Council, 1782, DesBarres Papers, Series III, p. 45.

ings obtained independently of the original surveys (for example by his assistant Knight), DesBarres performed a vital function and deserved the credit which he claimed.

His charts were only one instrumental part of the total war machine and on their own could be no guarantee of a British victory. On the other hand, they could and did save lives. Some testimony to this came from Hyde Parker (1739-1807) who was later to be the commander at Copenhagen when Nelson turned his famous blind eye. Parker was captain of the *Phoenix* in 1778 during a three-week storm so fierce that astronomical observations were impossible. The ship's officers believed that they were somewhere off Cape Cod but when soundings were taken and compared with DesBarres' charts it was discovered that they were approaching the dreaded Isle of Sable. An example of more general importance came from Howe's encounter with D'Estaing off Rhode Island in 1778. The British fleet had an advantage because not even the local American pilots could match the accuracy of the information DesBarres had provided. The war's fury and bloody glory thrust such unromantic matters as charts into the background but the naval commander in chief's concern indicates their value.[19]

Had the War of Independence not broken out, the chart maker's achievements might well have received both less and later recognition. The conflict gave him the opportunity to publish the *Neptune* with government subsidies. Even then the charts were so costly that private buyers were hard to find.[20] If it had not been for the chance offered by the Revolution, the manuscripts might not have survived the battles over DesBarres' possessions which embittered his later years and plagued his descendants long after his death. Sometimes the fury of war can hardly match a family's skirmishes! As it was, the charts became the standard guides for the navigation of the eastern coast of North America and were not improved upon until the works of Bay-

19. Histories of the naval side of the revolution pay little attention to the charts available for both sides. See, as examples, William M. James, *The British Navy in Adversity* (London, 1926), Alfred T. Mahan, *The Major Operations of the Navies in the War of Independence* (Boston, 1913), and William L. Clowes, *The Royal Navy* (7 vols.; London, 1897-1903), of which Volumes II and III are relevant to this period.

20. At The Hague, DesBarres had to offer the *Neptune* at a reduced price. See Isaac Stokes, *Iconography of Manhattan Island* (6 vols.; New York, 1915-28), I, 349.

field and Shortland nearly a century later.[21] In addition, his delicate watercolor views more than entitle DesBarres to be included among the century's minor artists.

On the charts subtle variations in shading showed differences in soil structures and types of beaches, and for major harbors special notes were given. A vital aid to navigation has to have considerable detail, but the number of soundings in a typical DesBarres chart was exceptional for his day. Their range is great, from a general outline of a large section of the America's Atlantic coastline or the whole coast of eastern Nova Scotia to elaborate studies of one harbor such as St. Mary's Bay, Nova Scotia. One of the quicker ways of detecting a chart not originally surveyed by DesBarres is to look at its detail. The one of Boston Harbor, principally based on the surveys of George Callendar in 1769, has many excellent features but there are no soundings for the Charles River and even more important entrances into the bay are left unnamed and unsounded. Another interesting aspect of the *Neptune* was the inclusion of a town plan of Newport, precursor of the truly massive one DesBarres made of Sydney, Cape Breton after he became governor.[22] A more confusing feature was DesBarres' tendency to put English names, including those of personal friends and national leaders, for local places. Many of these, unlike the ones which Holland used for Prince Edward Island, were not kept in later surveys. During the nineteenth century some of Des-Barres' soundings were shown to be inaccurate. Of course, all coast-lines change formation slightly, seabeds do not stay the same, and by the 1840's surveyors had better equipment and greater manpower, but the suspicion remains that DesBarres may have rushed one or two parts of his surveying to have more time for the artistic pleasure of making the charts.

21. Henry W. Bayfield began his surveys of the Gulf of St. Lawrence in 1828 and continued them until his promotion in 1856. New Brunswick was resurveyed in the 1840's by William Fitzwilliam Owen and Nova Scotia in the 1850's by Peter F. Shortland. See John C. Webster, *The Life of Joseph Frederick Wallet DesBarres* (Shediac, N. B., 1933), p. 28. Although responsible for the major correction of DesBarres' charts, Bayfield stated that for his time the earlier surveyor had been accurate, in respect to magnetic variation for example, *The St. Lawrence Pilot* (4th ed.; London, 1860), p. 14.

22. Now in the Map Division, PAC. DesBarres' skillful town planning is briefly described in Michael H. Brunt, "The Origin of Colonial Settlements in the Maritimes," *Plan*, I (1960), 102-04.

Hydrography was where he made his most important and lasting contribution. He shone in this area precisely in the way that he was later less than brilliant as a colonial administrator, that is in clearly formulating the task and executing it with a high degree of attention to detail. DesBarres made no vital advance in the theory of chart making but by developing existing techniques he was able to achieve new standards of precision, and by exercising innate artistic talents he built a glorious alliance between the accurate and the esthetic. Throughout what was always difficult and sometimes dangerous work, his dedication was apparent. Speaking of the obstacles which he faced, he made clear in the Preface to the *Atlantic Neptune* that he consciously sought a place in History—"when the author reflects that the accuracy and truth of his Work will stand the test of ages, and preserve future Navigators on that Coast, from the horror of shipwreck and destruction, he does not repine its having employed so large a portion of his Life." He achieved his goal.

CHAPTER III

Landlord in the Maritimes

MANY British officers in America during the eighteenth century tried their hand as entrepreneurs. Land was not only the most available commodity but also the most common symbol of social status, and so it was natural that land grants were what the military men were seeking. DesBarres, with his special knowledge of surveying and his considerable ambition, was hardly likely to be an exception to the general practice. In the years when he was mapping the coastline of Nova Scotia and adjoining areas, he purchased estates extensive enough to make him one of the largest landholders in the Maritimes.[1] As early as 1763 he became involved in a syndicate, of which Michael Francklin the lieutenant governor of Nova Scotia was the most prominent member, which sought a township grant of 100,000 acres on the promise of settling at least 100 Protestant families from Germany within five years.[2]

The petition was unsuccessful but in the next year or so members were given individual grants. DesBarres' was 20,000 acres at Tatamagouche on the northern shores of Nova Scotia, which he added to the 500 acres he held in Falmouth township (increased fourfold in 1768). In May 1765 he and six other men received a tract of land in Cumberland County and on it two estates were established. Minudie, of which DesBarres owned seven-eighths, was 8,000 acres in size and so rich in the highly fertile marshlands that he called it the Elysian Fields. The second estate, named Maccan-Nappan after the two little streams which ran through it, was roughly the same size and eventually was wholly owned by DesBarres. In 1775 he completed the purchase of two more farms, with a total acreage of nearly 40,000 acres, between the Memramcook and Petitcodiac rivers in the present province of New Brunswick. It is clear, therefore, that the decade spent in

1. After returning to Halifax in 1760 or 1761, he took the opportunity to scrutinize a number of areas while officially investigating the possibility of opening up further roads in the province. See "A Memorial of Major DesBarres," 1784, DesBarres Papers, Series V, p. 678.

2. On the syndicate, see Winthrop P. Bell, *The "Foreign Protestants" and the Settlement of Nova Scotia* (Toronto, 1961), p. 112, hereafter cited as Bell, *"Foreign Protestants."*

surveying was also a time of speculation and by its close the rising marine surveyor had title to immense estates. Since he was neither a scion of the aristocracy nor a member of a rich mercantile family, such impressive investments may seem suspicious.

Tatamagouche, the largest of his Nova Scotia estates, was a site chosen by himself at a cost of only the fees of the provincial officers and a small yearly quitrent.³ Similar expenses were involved in the Falmouth township land, and once he had received his grant in Cumberland County he was able to purchase nearby lands at very low prices.⁴ Careful investigation of his total holdings clears up the mystery of the lowly army officer turned large landowner. Nearly two-thirds of the land DesBarres held in 1773 had been obtained without any purchase capital and the remainder, roughly 14,000 acres, had been bought from prospectors whom he had aided with technical advice and from partners in his original grants. Many of them were not on the spot and were quite uninterested in Nova Scotia except as a side investment. DesBarres, on the other hand, had by a series of accidents found his career tied to work in the area. His assignment showed no signs of coming to a rapid completion just because the Admiralty was funding it inadequately. For a middle-aged man it made sense to purchase extensively in provinces where he had detailed information and sound governmental contacts. Yet Nova Scotia and New Brunswick, with the exception of the Bay of Fundy marshlands, were not noted for their soils and hardly comparable with lands available in the Thirteen Colonies. The result was that the Maritimes, then as now, were economically an inferior region and DesBarres was truth-

3. A copy of the Order in Council, July 11, 1764, which granted DesBarres his 20,000 acres at Tatamagouche is in DesBarres Papers, Series V, p. 2915. The order allowed him to select his tract in any part of the colony not already granted or surveyed, or claimed by Indians. In view of this order it is necessary to qualify the date, August 25, 1765, given by John C. Webster, *The Life of Joseph Frederick Wallet DesBarres* (Shediac, N. B., 1933), p. 65. It is possible that this later date refers to some other stage in the various legal procedures involved in a land grant.

4. In 1764, a grant of 1,000 acres did not cost more than £6 to "carry thro all the offices," Charles Morris, Jr. to DesBarres, March 23, 1774, DesBarres Papers, Series V, p. 495. The quitrent on the Tatamagouche grant was a farthing an acre. Nothing was to be paid for the first five years, half the total from the sixth to tenth year, and thereafter the full amount of £20.16s.8d. In February 1768, DesBarres bought 2,000 acres of the Minudie estate for £100 "currency in hand"; in April of 1769, he paid Alexander Morris £60 for each of two 1,000-acre lots in the Minudie grant. See ibid., pp. 2922, 2924, 2935, 2939 respectively.

fully able to report to fellow, but absent, grantees, that the estates were not yielding very much profit. They, in turn, were happy to sell an investment which had cost them little in initial capital but whose annual maintenance was relatively expensive.

An assumption that DesBarres cheated either persons or governments in order to make his purchases is neither necessary nor proven. With a salary of £365 every year, he had sufficient funds to establish his credit. In addition, he became well-known to Halifax mercantile houses, which were very dependent on government contracts, as he drew bills on the Admiralty for various expenses connected with his surveying. With cash, credit, and such references as the lieutenant governor, DesBarres was well able to buy broad estates. Naturally, he was intimately involved with government officials, especially those in the different land offices, but this was the inevitable result of both his professional work and his personal ambition.[5] While no one can believe that either civil or military officers in a British colony in the eighteenth century were a simon-pure lot, a reading of the lacunae in the records as proof of DesBarres' knavery is not only unjust but also silly because it flies in the face of the evidence we have and sensible reconstruction of his financial position.

Closer examination of DesBarres' estates presents a revealing picture of land acquisition and land policies in the North American colonies. The deportation of the Acadians in 1755 led to the reversion of large acreages to the Crown which, at the end of the Seven Years War, received a flood of petitions from both military men who wanted to settle in the region and civilians who saw opportunities for land speculation. Among these was the Philadelphia Company with, almost by definition, Benjamin Franklin among its most vigorous investors.[6] In such a competitive situation, DesBarres could balance a

5. Interesting details of the operation of the surveyor general's office and the loss of fees resulting from the Crown concessions to "reduced officers" will be found in the letter by Charles Morris, Jr., to DesBarres, March 23, 1774, ibid., p. 495 and in Morris to DesBarres, August 24, December 4, 1774, October 15, 1783, ibid., pp. 523, 531, 583.

6. Correspondence relating to the project will be found in the Hughes Papers, and there are a small number of reports by agents of the company in Ball Estate-Dupuy Papers. Both sets of papers are in the Hist. Soc. of Pennsylvania, Philadelphia. See Carl Van Doren, *Benjamin Franklin's Autobiographical Writings* (New York, 1945), pp. 649-50, and *Letters and Papers of Benjamin Franklin and Richard Jackson, 1753-1785* (Philadelphia, 1947), pp. 155, 157. See also William O. Sawtelle, "Acadia: The Pre-Loyalist Migration and the Philadelphia Plantation," *Pa. Mag. of Hist. and Biog.*, LI (1927), 244-89.

comparative lack of capital with an almost unrivaled technical competence. The result was that he did not do badly. Where he did not secure the richest lands, he was beaten out by people with either greater political pull or more money, but taking the economic possibilities of the colony as a whole his judgment was pretty sound. Tatamagouche, at the head of Amet Sound, was a key point on the route between Halifax and Charlottetown which would remain the seat of government in the island of Saint John (later Prince Edward Island) after the French were compelled to give it up in 1763. When DesBarres acquired his land the road already extended halfway across Nova Scotia, as far north as Truro. As for the Minudie and Maccan estates, they had already proved their richness under the hands of the Acadians who specialized in dyke agriculture. So DesBarres, with 40,000 acres even before he purchased the land on the western side of the Bay of Fundy, had extensive holdings and high expectations.

The lands never justified his hopes and, instead of providing profits to support his chart making enterprises and elevating him to the rank of a prominent landowner, proved to be continuous burdens. The exact interaction of the financial problems arising from his estates and those arising from his hydrographic, and later his governmental, services is a tricky matter. On the one hand, the Maritime holdings were a means of raising mortgages when DesBarres was in dire financial straits but, on the other, they tied up his money, established an unbreakable link with poverty-stricken colonies for someone who might have done better if he had been more free to pursue his career either in London or elsewhere in the British empire, and created a constant headache for both DesBarres and his family. In Nova Scotia tenants were hard to get, precious energies were dissipated in political quarrels, marketing facilities were poor, and DesBarres, as a landowner, was absent too long and too often, and always short of the capital and good management necessary for such large enterprises.

He looked to several sources for labor to work his estates. Wherever possible he tried to keep Acadian tenants, if there were any remaining, and sought to attract others where none were present.[7] DesBarres had

7. In 1764, the British government allowed Acadians to resettle in Nova Scotia provided they only resided in small groups scattered throughout the colony. The Nova Scotia authorities did not give them a fully legal position by making grants of land, so that their status was little better than that of squatters. See William S. McNutt, *New Brunswick, A History: 1784-1867* (Toronto, 1963), p. 6, hereafter cited as McNutt, *New Brunswick*.

the advantage of knowing French, and the Acadians in turn brought him the benefit of their experience in marsh farming. From time to time he added tenants from other groups. In 1771 he brought to his Tatamagouche estate a number of Montbéliardian families (people from his ancestral home) from among the "Foreign Protestants" settled at Lunenburg.[8] In the spring of the following year fifteen Yorkshire families settled on the Maccan and Nappan estates. Each family was allowed 200 acres at a rent of one penny per acre per annum for the first five years, sixpence from the sixth to the tenth year, and a shilling thereafter.[9] After the Revolution a few American refugees took leases on the DesBarres lands and some of them did quite well for themselves. William Pipes, for example, built a barn which cost at least one hundred and fifty pounds, and under his leadership the tenants built a bridge over the Nappan with the important result that the road from Halifax went through "the estate of Napan [sic] . . . instead of the former course by the ferry through Col. Barron's lands."[10]

The terms which DesBarres offered his tenants were not overly generous, but most were neither in a position to refuse nor able to pay cash rents. On most occasions he provided the livestock, with the tenants taking all the produce and the landlord receiving half of the annual increase in stock. Frequently he supplied the seed, and in return for this and his possession of the lands was supposed to obtain one-third of the grain harvest. DesBarres promised to provision his tenants should high tides break through the dykes. He also paid half the cost of building mills and obtained a quarter of the net profit. Although tenants could not transfer their lands without his consent, except to fellow tenants, DesBarres for his part was allowed to sell only after giving his tenants first option. These were the customary terms in the numerous agreements made, but DesBarres' absences and complex affairs caused many financial difficulties and frequent lawsuits which, in some cases, burdened his family for over half a century.[11]

8. Bell, *"Foreign Protestants,"* p. 552, n. 21a.

9. Captain John Macdonald made a report on the DesBarres estates (1795) which constitutes Series II of the DesBarres Papers. References will be given as Macdonald, Report (Tatamagouche), (Minudie), or (Maccan) as appropriate. On the terms granted the Yorkshire settlers, see Macdonald, Report (Maccan).

10. Macdonald, Report (Maccan).

11. This statement of terms is derived from scrutiny of a great number of agreements.

Between 1764 and 1773, while he himself was in the Maritimes, he appears to have expended considerable effort to attract tenants and consolidate his estates. At some time before 1768 he built a house, which he named Castle Frederick, on land in Falmouth township. His intention was to make this the "home farm" of his estates and also to use it during his winter's work of chart making.[12] When others, better placed to know and more astute in assessing political events, failed to perceive the full nature of American discontent, it was perhaps asking too much of DesBarres, always a very optimistic man, to pull in his financial horns. But, given the problems already encountered in meeting the expenses of the surveys, it was no stroke of financial genius to purchase more land after the American Revolution had broken out and his own estates in the Chignecto Bay region had been attacked by an expeditionary force from Machias, Maine. On top of this Des-Barres, even before he left Nova Scotia in 1773, had experienced tiresome legal disputes which plagued his estates throughout his ownership of them.

When DesBarres was in England, from 1773 to 1784, his Maritime investments sustained troubles from which he was never completely able to rescue them. Shortly before going home he overextended himself considerably by committing himself to the purchase of 30,000 acres from Joseph Goreham and 10,000 acres from Philip Skene. For these lands on the western side of the Bay of Fundy the price was £1,100 and £375 sterling respectively, with fees amounting to £100 for a total of £1,575 sterling or £1,750 Halifax currency.[13] Probably

Naturally, there were variations from time to time, but almost no differences in agreements made for the same estate at approximately the same time. Bell, *"Foreign Protestants,"* p. 551, charges that DesBarres was "intent on creating a manorial holding of European type." This conveys an incorrect impression. It is difficult to see that DesBarres could have sold land to Acadians who were so impoverished that they needed him to supply them with seed and stock. Richer groups, such as the Yorkshiremen, paid quitrents.

12. DesBarres had definitely established his residence as Castle Frederick by February 1768. See copy of bill of sale for lands at Minudie, February 2, 1768, in DesBarres, Papers, Series V, p. 2922. Other comments from the years before his return to England make it clear that he maintained residence there. See, for example, Charles Morris, Sr. to DesBarres, October 20, 1772, ibid., p. 433. For a time DesBarres employed Captain Rudolph Faesch as his agent. See Bell, *"Foreign Protestants,"* p. 317, n. 33a. In a letter to the author, Dr. Bell stated that DesBarres was in debt to Faesch, but finally paid off his bond. The suggestion may be a clue to another source of DesBarres' assets.

13. "Proposals for disposing of Petitcodiac and Memramcook," undated, in DesBarres Papers, Series V, p. 4462. The land had been valued at £7,500 currency when the sheriff attached it. See Joseph Goreham to DesBarres, April 15, 1776, ibid., p. 3303.

he intended to settle them with emigrants sent out by the Acadia Company, a British colonizing venture with which he had become connected, and there is a possibility that company funds were used for the purchase. The alluvial soils of the estates were certainly fertile, but trouble was brewing to the south and land was always on the market. In such circumstances, it was not a wise decision to double one's landholdings. We can only guess at DesBarres' reasons but he may have pinned his hopes to the company's schemes and the likelihood of bringing settlers over from Europe. Later on, when the success of the American Revolution was evident, he thought of selling or renting large sections of his lands to Loyalist refugees, but they obtained better terms from the government. In short, none of DesBarres' expectations was realized and the estates in New Brunswick eventually created his most extensive and expensive lawsuits.

Similar troubles with the Nova Scotia estates sprang from this same period. When he left in 1773 he could not be certain how long he would be away but his involvement with the *Neptune* and the war with the American colonies made it clear that he might be detained in London for a fairly long time. Formal provision for the administration of his estates became a necessity and in 1776 he appointed Mary Cannon and Edward Barron as agents for all of them. The letter of attorney to Cannon demanded that she should "act, transact, and perform all and every thing relative to my concerns, properties, and estates in my trust laying in the province of Nova Scotia."[14] With this loosely defined power she signed leases for DesBarres which he later repudiated on the grounds that she had no right to grant them. In the courts the many and protracted lawsuits often boiled down to the question of Cannon's authority to make such leases. Whatever the weaknesses of her management, and there seems little doubt that she was hardly competent to handle the involved problems DesBarres imposed upon her, she sought to protect the estates from being escheated and, in times of considerable difficulty, tried to keep the tenants moderately satisfied.[15] After all, it was DesBarres who was responsible for choosing her, probably since he was not going to take her back to London society

14. Power of Attorney, August 3, 1776, ibid., p. 4543. At the time the power was given, the New Brunswick estates were within the government of Nova Scotia.

15. There is testimony to the honesty of Cannon's agency in Richard Gibbons to DesBarres, September 5, 1775, November 2, 1783, ibid., pp. 614, 671.

and her services came cheaply, when others such as Charles Morris, Nova Scotia's surveyor general, were available. It was also his fault that the power of attorney was formulated in so general a fashion. His own absence, unavoidable though it may have been, hurt the chances of developing the estates and his unsatisfactory financial relationships with various government departments deprived him of capital and any clear picture of his prospects.

Appointment as lieutenant governor of Cape Breton in 1784 appeared to alter his position. Leaving England with nearly all accounts with the government advantageously settled, he could look forward to a new British government in an island close to his estates. As things turned out, the opportunity neither opened the way to a successful administrative career nor improved his financial standing. During his administration DesBarres incurred immense debts ultimately calculated in the tens of thousands of pounds. Some of these were with Halifax merchants, such as Samuel Sparrow, and these people, in touch with the local situation, endeavored to recoup at the expense of the estates. One of the most colorful incidents was the obtaining of a writ against the Tatamagouche estate and its enforcement by a sheriff who had to creep through the woods because the road from Halifax was still not completed. An embarrassed Mary Cannon wrote to DesBarres that "unless the cursed bills are paid the estates will be sold, as the Gentlemen at Law at Halifax hesitate not in giving judgement against you in any cause."[16]

Almost simultaneously legal storms were brewing in New Brunswick, which had become a separate colony in 1784. Within a month of his arrival the first governor, Thomas Carleton, issued a proclamation requiring all land previously received in a grant from the government of Nova Scotia to be registered anew. DesBarres failed to do this and so paved the way for later lawsuits by his tenants on the Memramcook and Petitcodiac estates. Although he was very busy in Cape Breton throughout his administration, it is surprising that he did not register his lands. A letter to a New Brunswick lawyer or a visit by Cannon would have been sufficient, if DesBarres felt he could not leave the island. There could hardly have been doubt that the registration would be carried through with little, if any penalty for nonfulfillment of the

16. Mary Cannon to DesBarres, November 22, 1788, ibid., p. 3366. Further details of Sparrow's actions will be found in ibid., pp. 1100-37, 1142, 1146-67, 1184-89, 1229.

grant's terms since the New Brunswick Council was proceeding slowly under instructions from the British government that escheat should occur only when the degree of neglect was excessive. Why DesBarres failed to meet the demands of the new order is not clear.[17] Perhaps it was simply the result of the same sort of inattention which happened during the period 1773-1784. Possibly he well understood the workings of an imperial policy which by 1790 still left nine-tenths of New Brunswick ungranted. Carleton did indeed turn a benign eye on Des-Barres' situation, but in Nova Scotia he was less kindly regarded. His administration of Cape Breton had aroused bitterness, particularly his accusations that the government at Halifax was jealous of his efforts to develop the island, and this was reflected in the unsympathetic manner with which his landholdings were treated. The period 1784-1787, far from establishing DesBarres as a brilliant governor and real estate investor, showed the weaknesses in his position and the deficiencies in the management of his lands.

It is apparent that the huge estates yielded DesBarres comparatively little in the way of profits. Tenants were hardly likely to develop the poor grade soil for an absentee landlord. Possibilities other than crop and animal farming were few and those that might have been open, such as timber sales, involved more capital than he had available, subjection to government regulation, investment in production facilities, and the finding of a ready market. Where tenants tried hard, and there were some like the Waugh family on the Tatamagouche estate who did, they were unhappy at sharing the fruits of their labors. The paying of rent was irksome and one tenant, Peter Maillard, expressed the general sense of irritation when he declared his readiness to "sell his whole little stock at once to pay it, in order to be free of duns for rent in future, however poorly he might live."[18] Many complained that the rents were too high, and some sought opportunities elsewhere yet, surprisingly, most came back to DesBarres' estates.[19] The owner's

17. McNutt, *New Brunswick*, p. 56 is misleading in his statement that DesBarres was "absent in England and failed to obey the regulation." It is true that Carleton arrived in New Brunswick before DesBarres reached Cape Breton, but there was an interval before he engaged Ward Chipman, Sr., to look into the question of the land grants. There was another interval before Chipman's report was ready, and after the first proclamation by Carleton of the need to re-register grants, a year's grace was given to holders of Nova Scotia grants.

18. Macdonald, Report (Tatamagouche).

19. On the richer intervale farms at Tatamagouche the rents were only 1s. for each of

gubernatorial troubles also hurt some tenants. They found themselves for a time with the public creditor as their landlord and he was not ready, as DesBarres had been, to accept their notes in lieu of the arrears of rents. Indeed, the quality of the soil, the type of farming, the technical skill of the settlers, the level of management, and the overall state of the economy added up to something less than a prepossessing picture. On a relative or competitive basis, marks in favor of any particular landlord's estates as Captain John Macdonald, one of Des-Barres' numerous agents, reported in 1795, were "founded upon the confidence in the owner, upon the general ideas of encouragement, justice, and security," except where there were significant differences in fertility.[20]

A useful indicator of the general economic level is the commonness of rent payments in kind. It is clear that DesBarres' tenants were living in little more than a barter market in a province where poor transportation facilities made it difficult to take advantage of the opportunities offered by Halifax with its sizable military, commercial and administrative communities. In addition, the incentive for greater productivity was blunted for tenants who had to pay their landlord fifty percent of any natural increase in the number of animals and a third of the grain crop. Tenant lawsuits in fact were concerned with obtaining release from the terms of their leases but when they tried to buy themselves out for any amounts up to the sum which would have yielded interest equal to the rent, they could not raise the cash. In effect, DesBarres was investing more and more money each year in his estates as he extended credit to his defaulting tenants and each "loan" made it all the harder for them to meet his selling price and for him to sell at a loss. External factors worsened the situation. Especially after 1787 DesBarres was under mounting pressure to clear off debts incurred in his public careers, and although his charts were easily his most valuable assets his claim to them was disputed. Both he

---

the first six years, but they climbed steeply to 20s. in the seventh year, £5 in the eighth year, £20 in the ninth year, and £27 for the tenth and subsequent years. All sums were calculated in sterling. DesBarres expected nine Acadian tenants to share the rent. When only four lots were taken up, the maximum rent was reduced to £20. "Tatamagouche Accounts with tenants, 1771-1786," DesBarres Papers, Series V, p. 3241, and DesBarres to James Langille, August 19, 1786, ibid., p. 3672. See also Macdonald, Report (Tatamagouche), which clearly shows the individual variations in rent.

20. Macdonald, Report (Tatamagouche).

and his creditors had hopes based on his estates, but he could neither sell in Britain for a price which covered his outlay nor find sufficient purchasers on the lands themselves. He could not return to Nova Scotia to take charge of his affairs because of the need to remain in London to fight legal cases involving large public debts which would become much needed personal capital should he ever be given unqualified ownership of the *Atlantic Neptune*.

As a man of science and the intimate of many officers and gentlemen interested in agriculture and land development, DesBarres was obviously aware of the agronomic advances made in England and America during the eighteenth century. Macdonald acidly expressed the opinion that it was a pity the owner's engineering genius had not been consistently applied to such problems as drainage in the areas of dyke farming, but he had to admit that greater fertility permitted two or three tons of hay to be cut in a day at Minudie while on his own estate on Saint John's Island he barely harvested one ton in two or three days. Reflecting the emphasis on balanced agriculture which had grown in England under the leadership of such famous gentlemen as Coke of Holkham and "Turnip" Townshend, he suggested using the marsh hay as feed for cattle whose dung would aid the growing of corn on the uplands. Such scientific farming required a fair amount of capital, a commodity which in DesBarres' case was never available in anything like adequate quantities. It also demanded an informed landlord on the estates or a knowledgeable agent. Unfortunately, the landlord was absent and the agent was ignorant.

Through all his financial predicaments DesBarres tried to provide the necessary investment. He claimed to have spent more than twenty-five thousand pounds on Minudie alone between 1766 and 1774.[21] On another occasion he declared that by 1813 more than fifty thousand pounds had been expended on the estates as a whole, but in a second calculation this amount was reduced to less than forty thousand pounds.[22] Exact computation was difficult, and so is any precise comment on DesBarres' claims since many of the figures for his expendi-

21. Outlays at Minudie, 1766-1774, DesBarres Papers, Series V, p. 3110. A series of small accounts for Minudie, many in French and most without dates, can be found in ibid., pp. 3123-85. In general they are from the period before 1795.

22. Tables in ibid., pp. 5166-75. DesBarres claimed that he spent nearly £30,000 on the New Brunswick estates between 1775 and 1813. See ibid., pp. 3623-27.

tures are not contemporary with those for his income. He also included cumulative interest charges and in some tabulations incorporated both the capital and the interest on the rents of his frequently defaulting tenants. The rent rolls, although large in quantity, are not very much more trustworthy. Here again the gaps in what is extant, the partial accounts, and the poor bookkeeping produce a confusing picture. Fairly typical figures are those for 1795-1796 when Minudie yielded a rent of just over one hundred pounds, Maccan-Nappan seventy-seven pounds, Tatamagouche thirty-eight pounds, and the lands in New Brunswick one hundred and six pounds.[23] But there was really no guarantee that rents would be paid either when they were due or later. One could take almost any year of DesBarres' ownership and find that arrears greatly exceeded the amounts received. On the Mem-ramcook-Petitcodiac estates in New Brunswick there were nearly as many people paying their dues in kind as there were persons charged with rent. However, eviction was not the answer to the landlord's problems since tenants were not easy to find and whatever the difficulties it was always better to have the lands cultivated in some fashion than to let them return entirely to waste. The conclusions are that Des-Barres did not spend as much on the estates as he claimed he did, received only a fraction of the profits he expected, and over the years lost considerable sums of money.

The estates were further burdened because of the lawsuits they engendered. The causes were primarily DesBarres' absences and his lack of capital which led to such problems as boundary disputes, failure to register the lands, incomplete and imprecise directions to agents, and general tenant dissatisfaction. An early example is the dispute with George Adam Gemelin. In the Trinity term of 1769 the chief justice of Nova Scotia awarded DesBarres one hundred and eighty pounds sixteen shillings and sixpence plus costs against Gemelin in settlement of a debt. A writ was served on Gemelin's holding, lying in the Maccan and Nappan valleys. When the estate was put up at auction, DesBarres was the highest bidder and thereby obtained a large tract of good land for the comparatively low price of two hundred and twenty pounds. Judgment, writ, and purchase were all perfectly proper at a time and place where land speculators rarely bothered about legal niceties.

23. Rent rolls, ibid., pp. 4253-55, 4290.

Nevertheless, the incident reveals the litigious and uncharitable side of DesBarres' nature and suggests how closely ambition and avarice sometimes run together. Over the long haul he benefited little. Gemelin contested the purchase and began a battle which lasted two decades before the case was taken over by the township of Amherst which conducted an even more vigorous action to invalidate DesBarres' claim. In 1792 Edward Barron, after finding that Cumberland County court was satisfied that the land belonged to Amherst, expressed the opinion that when DesBarres "is properly inform'd of the . . . circumstances he will I think decline any further pursuit about it."[24] It was a poor estimate. Aided by the Morrises, both father and son, who as surveyors general of Nova Scotia had access to the land records, the legal wars were kept going for the rest of DesBarres' long life. The contentious plaintiff did little to help those hired to help him and before his death had run through a string of attorneys. He constantly failed to provide them with the papers they needed. Some had been lost during his disjointed career between 1764 and 1787 and others he was loath to send over from England once he had seen twin copies of official dispatches from his administration of Cape Breton lost by British bureaucrats who then waited twenty years before admitting it. An additional reason for his attitude sprang from his incurable optimism which each year convinced him that British ministries, bogged down in the Revolutionary and Napoleonic Wars, would find time to solve his claims. In the meantime the estates stagnated, the tenants groused, and the lawyers despaired either of winning the cases or receiving their fees.

Over the years DesBarres used the services of a number of people, but the most important was Mary Cannon. She served the longest and controlled the farms during the period which was critical in bringing about their decline. She was ill rewarded for her loyalty. When lawsuits seriously hurt the estates after 1790 DesBarres, who had seen little of Cannon during the time he was governor of Cape Breton Island, turned on her and harshly blamed her for his losses and his legal entanglements. The fault was really his as much as hers. At issue were the powers of attorney he had given Cannon in 1776 and in 1784, under which she had granted leases and a number of con-

24. Edward Barron to Mary Cannon, April 29, 1792, ibid., p. 3381.

cessions to the tenants.[25] DesBarres wanted the leases sent on to him for his approval but he neglected to return them to the agent who nevertheless, either at his direction or more probably on her own initiative, included a clause reserving DesBarres' right to disavow the contract.

His failure to respond placed her in a very invidious position. The lands must be managed as if the leases were in application, although without DesBarres' consent this was not really the case. Yet since she appeared to have the right as agent to execute whatever actions or transactions were necessary with respect to the holdings, it might seem that this included the power to draw up terms for tenants. In fact, the letters of attorney and the whole history of the estates raised many interesting legal problems. Even if Cannon had acted without sufficient authority, did not the receiving of rent involve acquiescence and constitute acceptance of the leases granted? Could the leases be good to recover rent and void as to the tenure of the lessees? Could the tenants be evicted? Did they not have the right, regardless of the Cannon leases, of staying on the lands because they had paid rents? Should they be evicted, was it not likely that they could obtain a Chancery decision compelling the landlord to pay for improvements made under his acquiescence? It hardly seemed that any of these questions, except possibly the last (and that only if the validity of his accounts were proven), would be answered in favor of DesBarres.

In New Brunswick there was at least as much danger of escheat since the colony had been established after the American Revolution and settled by land-hungry Loyalists, who included a fair sprinkling of shrewd lawyers. DesBarres' laxity about registering the lands provided excellent grounds for legal action by tenants who were not substantially better off than those in Nova Scotia, but the owner proved himself no fool in the arts of judicial delay. He hired well-placed attorneys, such as Amos Botsford and Ward Chipman (father and son), who operated in a colony where both the governor and the council were sympathetic to the interests and difficulties of landowners, even absent ones.[26] Yet DesBarres was almost extraordinarily lucky.

25. DesBarres to Cannon, May 18, 1776, January 19, 1784, ibid., pp. 3426, 4543. See also power of attorney for Memramcook and Petitcodiac, August 3, 1776, quoted in Amos Botsford to James L. DesBarres, December 8, 1805, ibid., 3720.

26. Both Mary Cannon and Amelia DesBarres told DesBarres that despite a petition

He ignored the advice of his lawyers, compelling Botsford to describe him as "a gentleman who seems to pay no attention to his business," and year in year out omitted to pay them their promised fees even though, with all the obstacles he placed in their way, they did well by him. In 1802 a ruling in the New Brunswick Supreme Court ordered his tenants to pay their long accumulated rent arrears and recommended a new grant of the thirty thousand acres he had purchased from Joseph Goreham nearly forty years previously. DesBarres immediately told Botsford to obtain a similar decision for the adjoining ten thousand acres he owned.[27] To issue an order was one thing, but to execute it quite another in a colony where police work was an amateur and local matter.

For nearly half a century the lands were a source of losses and litigation. DesBarres even offered to sell them to the tenants but on terms in which a first condition was the payment of rent arrears. More active and prosperous tenants took their own legal proceedings, seeking a writ of *scire facias,* an instrument based on the original charter and subsequent agreements, which would direct the sheriff to demand that the landlord show cause why his opponents should not have the advantage and obtain repeal of the Crown grant and annulment of the record. The case was a morass, with charges and counter charges on both legal details and on the question of who had made what improvements in keeping with contracts whose validity both DesBarres and the tenants disputed.[28] On both sides there was irascibility and irrationality. A greedy landlord had overreached himself in his initial purchases, provided inadequate incentive to tenants who were not among the most enterprising, complicated matters still further by a tangled web of finances arising from public careers, and failed to pay

from four tenants at Petitcodiac, Governor Carleton did not intend to escheat any of the lands in his province, Mary Cannon to DesBarres, December 6, 1789, Amelia DesBarres to DesBarres, December 10, 1789, DesBarres Papers, Series V, pp. 3404, 3405.

The Provincial Secretary, Jonathan Odell, informed DesBarres' lawyer that "the rule of this Government had been not to carry the Act of Assembly into rigid execution unless where either the lands have been uncultivated or complaints had been exhibited against the grantee by the occupants and actual cultivators." Jonathan Odell to Ward Chipman, Sr., March 25, 1795, ibid., p. 3776.

27. Botsford to DesBarres, August 10, 1802, and DesBarres to Botsford, March 1, 1803, ibid., pp. 3708, 3710.

28. Copy of memorial, July 14, 1812, in ibid., p. 4536. Opinion by Richard Uniacke, November 1, 1800, ibid., p. 4105.

enough attention to local advice. The estates were a natural product of DesBarres' technical skills and the social values of his century, but in trying to combine extensive landholding with hydrography and colonial administration he stretched his resources and energies almost to the breaking point.

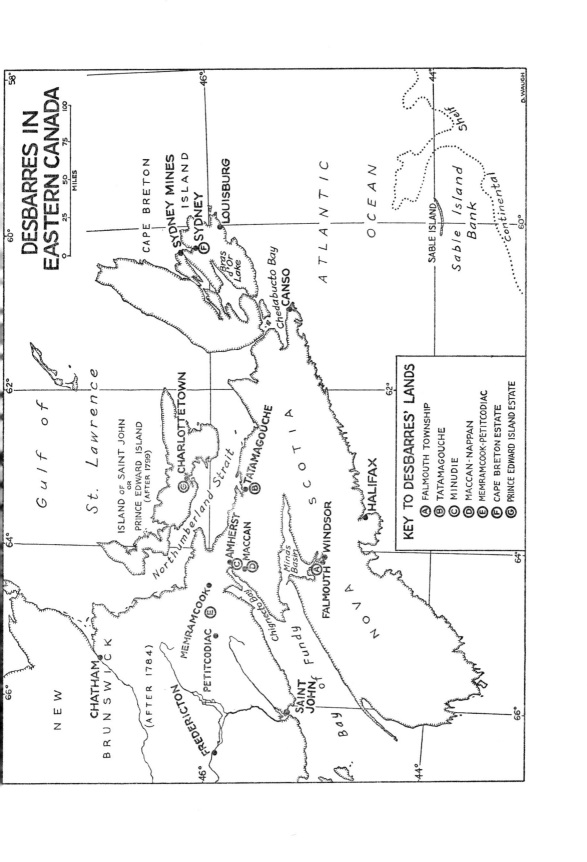

DESBARRES IN EASTERN CANADA

O. WAUGH

MILES
0 25 50 75 100

KEY TO DESBARRES' LANDS

- Ⓐ FALMOUTH TOWNSHIP
- Ⓑ TATAMAGOUCHE
- Ⓒ MINUDIE
- Ⓓ MACCAN-NAPPAN
- Ⓔ MEMRAMCOOK-PETITCODIAC
- Ⓕ CAPE BRETON ESTATE
- Ⓖ PRINCE EDWARD ISLAND ESTATE

ATLANTIC OCEAN

Gulf of St. Lawrence

NEW BRUNSWICK

(AFTER 1784)

CHATHAM

FREDERICTON

MEMRAMCOOK ⒺPETITCODIAC

SAINT JOHN

Bay of Fundy

Minas Basin

Chignecto Bay

ⒸAMHERST
ⒹMACCAN

Ⓐ FALMOUTH WINDSOR

HALIFAX

NOVA SCOTIA

Northumberland Strait

ⒼCHARLOTTETOWN

ISLAND OF SAINT JOHN
OR
PRINCE EDWARD ISLAND
(AFTER 1799)

ⒷTATAMAGOUCHE

CAPE BRETON

ISLAND

SYDNEY MINES
ⒻSYDNEY
LOUISBURG

Bras D'or Lake

Chedabucto Bay
CANSO

SABLE ISLAND

Sable Island Bank

Continental Shelf

CHAPTER IV

Little Isle of Trouble

HIS first administrative position came to DesBarres at the age of sixty-two, old by the standards of either this or his own century. No one could foresee that the doughty gentleman would continue to be a thorn in bureaucracy's hide for another four decades! His training prior to 1784, when he took up his duties as governor of Cape Breton, had not particularly equipped him for the job. Successively army officer, engineer, quartermaster, marine surveyor and landlord, he had handled small groups of men but never directed administrative machinery or executed imperial policies. But the island with a population of little more than a thousand demanded no more experience than DesBarres had to offer, and he could certainly claim that hardly anyone knew the region better.[1] When it seemed desirable to remove from Whitehall's anterooms someone who could win prizes as the most prolix and persistent of petitioners, the bleak isle appeared a fitting place to put him.[2]

For some two hundred years Cape Breton had been a French possession. After the War of the Spanish Succession or Queen Anne's War (1702-1713), money was poured into the colony to build the gray bastion of Louisbourg and turn the island into the Gibraltar of the Gulf. It held control over the Atlantic approach to French Canada and stood guard over rich fishing grounds and important colonial trade. In 1758 it fell to the British and was ceded to them in the peace treaty five years later. By the time DesBarres became its governor the whole valley of the St. Lawrence and the lands around the Gulf were in British hands, so the strategic value of Cape Breton had decreased. Annexed to Nova Scotia, of which it has formed a part ever since except for the period of thirty-six years initiated by DesBarres' administration, it was a little place in imperial plans and could be left to languish.

1. The size of the population in 1774 is given in Public Archives of Nova Scotia, hereafter PANS, XLIV, Document 48, tabled in Daniel C. Harvey (ed.), *Holland's Description of Cape Breton* (Halifax, 1935), p. 11.

2. The main recommendation of DesBarres came from General Conway, a former Secretary of State. See Thomas Steele to William Henry Cavendish Bentinck, 3d Duke of Portland, June 16, 1801, DesBarres Papers, Series III, p. 219.

There was no real attempt to develop its resources in timber, coal, and fish, despite the pleas of both the merchant and governing classes in Halifax.

The island suffered in its own way from the generally restrictive policies of the British government between 1763 and 1776. The potential revenues of the mines belonged to the King, to be made actual at his pleasure.[3] No opportunity, even a peripheral one, must be given the American colonials to disobey the prohibitions on the manufacture of iron, although in practice they were very profitably doing precisely this.[4] On Cape Breton no permanent land grants could be made either to residents or intending immigrants. The island did not even have parliamentary representation. In 1770 the House of Assembly at Halifax salved its conscience on this point by invoking the doctrine of "virtual representation," at the very time it was under violent attack by the lawyer-politicians in the Thirteen Colonies.[5] In short, the colony was an excellent example of a British policy of neglect which was never in any way salutary since, unlike the American colonies, local resources could not be developed by a minuscule population. The whole island was reserved for the Crown in 1774 but in the next year a hurried alteration in policy allowed the governor of Nova Scotia to grant lands to American refugees and to encourage timber and coal exports to the West Indies. Although there was some use of Cape Breton fuel for the garrisons at Louisbourg and Halifax during the American Revolution, no important changes in the state of the island occurred.

In 1784 the old Acadia was broken into three parts, the colonies of New Brunswick, Nova Scotia, and the subordinate territory of Cape Breton. The basis for the division was partly administrative conve-

---

3. For the Nova Scotia case see Michael Francklin to Board of Trade, September 30, 1766, PANS, XXXVII, Document 54, and Lord William Campbell to Shelburne, February 27, 1767, ibid., XLIII, Document 1. Shelburne's reply is in ibid., XXXI, Document 64. The argument for reservation to the King is made in Lords of the Treasury to the King, October 28, 1766, Colonial Office 5, America and West Indies (Public Archives of Canada transcripts), hereafter C. O. 5 (PAC transcripts), LXVII, 195.

4. Lords of the Treasury to the King, October 28, 1766, ibid., LXVII, 20. See also a typical letter prohibiting mining, Lord Dartmouth to Governor Legge, January 27, 1775, Dartmouth Papers (PAC transcripts), I, 1095.

5. In December, 1787, Stephen Cottrell, writing for the Committee for Trade of the Privy Council to Governor Macarmack, complained that the Acts of the Assembly were not being sent in their proper form. See PANS, CCCXV, Document 17. Yet there had not been an Assembly on the island!

nience and partly the need to proliferate offices for the incoming Loyalists. Cape Breton was clearly the least valuable and in practice it was almost independent since John Parr, the governor of Nova Scotia, hardly communicated with his lieutenant in Sydney some two hundred and forty miles away. Nova Scotia had lands available for the Loyalists and, although there were strained relations between the old settlers and the newcomers, the turbulence of their influx was alleviated. In New Brunswick they had the colony almost to themselves and in it found fertile valleys. DesBarres had the hardest job of all. In his province good land was scarce, but the British government prevented the colonists from making up for this by mining the rich coal seams and when it came to reaping the harvests from the bountiful fishing grounds, the established fleets of Britain, New England, and Nova Scotia held the advantage.

The first, and thereafter the central, question for the governor was how to feed settlers in an island whose soil could barely support them when they had not been there long enough to raise sufficient crops for themselves. He had to face, on behalf of all the inhabitants, a simple yet critical fact: farming requires considerable capital if only in the form of time. DesBarres didn't have an entirely free hand because he was responsible to Parr. His colony was at the mercy of Halifax merchants for supplies of badly needed consumer and capital goods. His administration was forced to find room for two ambitious and aggrieved Loyalists. The first, David Mathews, had briefly been mayor of New York and the second, the more able Abraham Cuyler, had become mayor of Albany at the age of twenty-eight.

In 1778 his strong Loyalist sympathies had forced Cuyler to flee to Lower Canada where he served effectively as Inspector General of Refugees.[6] As the end of the war drew near he decided to move to Cape Breton instead of joining the refugees whom he had helped to resettle. His plans were to take with him about six hundred Loyalists who would form the nucleus of a new settlement and be personally obligated to him. Apparently he assessed the economic opportunities of the island favorably, but there can be little doubt that to the one-

6. The attacks on Cuyler in James Sullivan (ed.), *Minutes of the Albany County Committee of Correspondence, 1775-1778* (2 vols.; Albany, 1923-25), I, 402, 405. The committee sent Cuyler and others to Hartford, Connecticut, in the belief that there they would be less of a danger, *ibid.*, I, 445, 457, 459.

time mayor it also seemed a pliant fiefdom.[7] On at least one occasion he sought the whole colony for himself and his group.[8] The appointment of DesBarres was a blow to his pride and matters were not helped when the new governor, making use of his vast knowledge of the coast, decided to create a new center of government not at Louisbourg where Cuyler was living rather miserably, but at Spanish River with the fine, deep anchorages of Sydney Harbor.[9] Governor and Secretary therefore did not work together during their first few months on the island and the new administration was off to a less than brilliant start.

During the winter of 1784-1785 little progress in the development of the settlement could be made. Everyone was too busy keeping their crude shelters intact and their stomachs partly filled. The failure of the British government to provide either adequate funds for the colony or immediate and sufficient sustenance for the settlers was the prime cause of DesBarres' problems, and the ultimate reason for both his recall and the reopening of a protracted legal battle with successive British ministries. Only two things were at all clear. The arrangements for the Loyalists were to be the same as in Nova Scotia, and the government and officers were to take the same fees as their counterparts in Halifax. Hardly enough. Of what value were precise regulations as to what provisions the Loyalists were entitled to have without providing them or money for their speedy purchase? The Halifax merchants were busy supplying the refugees in their own colony, and there were several thousands of them.[10] Cape Breton was an isolated and poor colony, not a place to attract shipments from England simply on the basis of possible profit. Seemingly, the only method was dependence on the governor's personal credit and the continued neglect of the imperial government quickly forced him to extend this far beyond his means of repayment. The colony needed extensive and well-

7. At the same time he was very conscious of the remoteness of Canada from the existing commercial markets and the sparsity of its population. His conclusion was that costs would be high and opportunities for trade few. Cuyler to Haldimand, August 18, 1783, Haldimand Papers (PAC transcripts), CLXV, 114.

8. See his "Proposals relative to Cape Breton," in ibid., CLXV, 263.

9. Cuyler to Nepean, March 11, 1784 in Original Correspondence, Secretary of State—Cape Breton, Colonial Office 217, hereafter C. O. 217.

10. Governor Parr estimated in September 1783, that 18,000 Loyalists had come into Nova Scotia. By April 1, 1784, the number had reached 30,000. Parr to Haldimand, September 30, 1783, April 1, 1784, Haldimand Papers (PAC transcripts), CXLIX, 301, 321.

directed support. What it received was a pittance for contingent expenses and the salaries of half a dozen officials. Poor, jealous of richer Nova Scotia, unable to exploit its resources, it was almost bound to be a trouble spot.

This was not the view of the new governor. Much of the credit for bringing the settlers through their first winter belongs to him, although at times he allowed his natural optimism to become so inflated it was outlandish. An example is his claim that "the value of property in this island must in a very little time far exceed that of any others in America."[11] In the summer of 1785 plans were made to carve the new town of Sydney out of the wilderness; for this the governor was able to get help from six companies of the 33d regiment, the island's garrison. DesBarres did not know it, but it was the beginning of his troubles with the military. He must have been more aware of the threat posed by Cuyler who had been given the powerful and potentially profitable posts of clerk of the council, secretary of the island, and registrar of grants, deeds, and conveyances. The American was soon at loggerheads with his leader and felt it necessary to send Under Secretary of State Evan Nepean a letter vindicating his conduct at Louisbourg and complaining about some of DesBarres' appointments. In a tiny colony everyone knew each other's business and Cuyler's irritation could not have remained a secret very long.

Such signs of disputation were the more difficult to bear since Cape Breton's economy seemed to be improving a little. During the summer of 1785 almost seventy ships came to the three ports of Sydney, St. Peter's, and Conway (Île Madam), taking away some 22,500 quintals (approximately 1,125 tons) of fish, 234 barrels of oil, 1,199 chaldrons (approximately 1,538 tons) of coal, and over 400 skins. In addition, more than a hundred little boats or shallops had been made by the settlers for fishing the inshore waters. Sydney was slowly being built and it was hoped that the governor and the officers and men of the regiment would be "very comfortably lodged" by September. DesBarres' belief that it would become an "opulent fishing town" might yet be vindicated. These prospects were not fulfilled. During the bitterly cold days of winter, passions became inflamed and tempers raised to boiling point. The reason was terrifyingly simple: the settle-

11. DesBarres to Roberts [his agent], August 3 and 9, 1785, C. O. 217.

ment faced starvation. Hungry men will hardly arrive at a fair verdict but the historian has a better chance. In answering the question of whether the governor was guilty of criminal neglect, we have to discover what he had done to avert the crisis, whether responsibility for doing so lay solely with him and, after the shortage had been realized, how he handled the problem.

DesBarres cannot be blamed for ignoring the needs of the settlers. He recognized the importance of acquiring sufficient provisions for the winter as early as June 1785, and asked Gregory Townsend, the colony's agent in Halifax, to obtain food for about a thousand people for six months, together with two puncheons (large casks) of rum and four hogsheads of molasses for distribution to those laboring on the public works.[12] The reply came back that neither the civil governor, Parr, nor the military commander, Campbell, had "any orders or instructions to send any provisions or stores from this place to your government," and that even if such directives had been received all available supplies were required for the Loyalists in Nova Scotia.[13] The stores sent to Parr were for the troops, disbanded army corps, and Loyalists in Nova Scotia and New Brunswick. If, as seemed the case, Whitehall had forgotten Cape Breton, the governor would have to rely on human kindness, his own ingenuity and, ultimately, reappraisal of the situation by the authorities at home.

For the rest of the summer DesBarres went ahead with plans to procure supplies, but not surprisingly his credit did not prove very acceptable in Halifax. Townsend said that he could not "obtain a shilling of public money" without Campbell's consent. On the very same day that he was telling the governor his bills were not negotiable, a London trading company informed him it had made a contract with the imperial government to supply provisions for the troops in Nova Scotia and its dependencies and the Treasury had expressly ordered that the supplies for Cape Breton and the Island of Saint John be sent direct.[14] Campbell also relented somewhat and gave a warrant to meet the cost of flour which was to be issued by John Storey, an assistant

12. Benjamin Lovell to Gregory Townsend, June 6, 1785, Col. Corresp., Cape Breton (PAC transcripts), LXIII.

13. Townsend to DesBarres, July 6, 1785, C. O. 217.

14. Turnbull Macaulay and T. Gregory to DesBarres, July 6, 1785, C. O. 217. This company is usually referred to as Turnbull and Macaulay and was so called by Gregory Townsend. The letter of this date, however, was written over the signature as given here.

dispatched to Sydney by Townsend. Toward the end of August 1785 a letter was sent by Campbell's secretary to Colonel Yorke, the senior officer with the troops on the island, asking for a listing of the military staff and promising provisions for every officer holding his commission from the War Office. All the military, including the Town Adjutant, Barracks Master, Commissary of Stores and Provisions, Chaplain, and Surgeon were to be subordinate to the "officer commanding the troops in the said island in subordination to the general." But DesBarres claimed that as governor he was also the island's commander in chief. The dispute was further complicated by the inclusion of some of the military officers on DesBarres' Council and the practical involvement of all responsible men, in uniform or not, in the affairs of the tiny colony. Some conflict between the civil and the military was almost unavoidable.

The governor spent the last months of the summer and the early fall of 1785 in a continued search for supplies. He sent Thomas Venture as a personal emissary to Halifax, but he had no luck against bureaucratic obstinacy and the agent's indifference. Venture moved on to the American states where he picked up a small amount of provisions and a large number of promises from intending immigrants.[15] Townsend, as late as October, could offer no better news than that he had been mistaken in thinking that the supplies sent there for troops and Loyalists included a portion for settlers on Cape Breton. Finally Samuel Sparrow, a Halifax merchant, was persuaded to place an agent at Sydney to whom DesBarres gave bills on the Treasury worth more than three thousand pounds.

By the winter the situation was very unsatisfactory. Totally inadequate supplies for the young colony had been sent from Britain. In Nova Scotia the merchants had their hands full meeting the needs of the Loyalists there and generally did what the military and civil officials told them to do. The island's agent was unimaginative and uncooperative and its governor was deeply in debt. As the man on the spot the dire need of Cape Breton's people struck DesBarres hardest and so, with a mixture of compassion and cavalier disregard for established procedures, he strayed beyond the strict bounds of his Instruc-

---

15. A proclamation by DesBarres, a copy of which was presumably given to Venture, noted the prospects for a rich fishing industry and declared that the island was "peculiarly adapted for establishing the whale fishery on the largest scale."

tions. Yet perhaps such a course was wise. Ignoring for the moment the simple humaneness of his policies, the future even the survival of the colony was at stake and in the long run it was this for which a governor would be held accountable. In handling the impending food crisis Des-Barres may not have demonstrated the finesse or effectiveness of a born administrator, but his measures had been creditable attempts in a very difficult position. He dealt with the second large problem bequeathed him by Whitehall, the poorly delineated powers of the civil and the military authorities, in a less praiseworthy fashion.

The quarrel came into the open on November 2, 1785. Colonel Yorke, the commander of the local garrison, replied to a message from DesBarres by quoting lengthy passages from a letter written by General Campbell's secretary. He had been ordered to tell the governor that:

Notwithstanding provisions coming out consigned to Governors (in consequence of an imitation of the old practice of office) yet invariably they are understood by letters from Ministry to be received by, and immediately under the controul of the Military Department in this country, and that the General therefore requires an observance of the same rule in the Island of Cape Breton. . . . The General consequently expects that provisions that may arrive in whatever manner they may be consigned for whomsoever intended are to be put in charge of the Acting Commissary to be issued by your directions as Military Commanding Officer.[16]

Although Yorke could do nothing but obey, DesBarres had no such duty. He reported to Governor Parr, he was responsible for the whole island, he envisioned a rapidly developing colony. Settlers would certainly not be attracted if a picture of military control became broadcast. To Yorke he replied with copies of various documents including a letter from the War Office, which in his view conclusively proved his right to control the issuing of provisions.[17]

If it had not been that many lives were in jeopardy, the skirmishes among the governor, the colonel, and their subordinates during the winter of 1785-1786 would have many of the characteristics of opera bouffe. Each side was equally authoritarian and uncompromising. Typical of the silly pettiness was the first confrontation, an attempt to

16. Enclosure in Yorke to DesBarres, November 2, 1785, C. O. 217.
17. DesBarres to Yorke, November 3, 1785, C. O. 217.

get the key to the store in which Storey was holding the provisions. On this matter as on most of the incidents, the Council did not give the governor very much support.[18] DesBarres found his only stalwart defender in the Chief Justice, Richard Gibbons.[19] In the next month two military officers on the Council resigned and were joined by David Mathews, who became increasingly useful in providing Yorke and Cuyler with legal arguments to counter those given the governor by Gibbons. In a small colony whose very survival was in the balance, the chief officers were being split into defenders and opponents of the governor. Clearly, rigidity and righteousness were being substituted for common sense and compromise.

DesBarres did his share in creating such an atmosphere. While, on the one hand, the governor had to deal with a colonel who had little power to negotiate but an overriding duty to obey an absent general, on the other he reasserted his stubborn and self-righteous personality and frequently appeared to be demanding an agreement solely on his terms. Late in November 1785 he missed a chance to keep the various groups together, simultaneously seeming to show more concern for his powers than the fate of those over whom he exercised them. DesBarres rejected a request for assistance in recovering stores from the wrecked *President* because they were to be placed in the charge of Storey, the military commissary officer. He added that "in the case of these provisions, Government could not be left at a loss, for they are the property of the contractors . . . and therefore the loss will fall on the insurers, for whose benefit steps shall be taken as the law provides." This irrelevant legalism scarcely benefited the starving settlers. DesBarres blamed Yorke for hindering the growth of the island's population, in this comment presumably thinking of the colony's "image" to prospective colonists. Finally, the governor poured scorn on the colonel's reference in an earlier letter, to what "you are pleased to call an Extract of your Instructions exhibiting a frivolous recital of extracts of correspondence between the brigade major and yourself, between the contractor's agent and the brigade major, between

18. Cape Breton, Executive Council Minutes, November 18, 1785, hereafter Cape Breton B.

19. Gibbons became Attorney General of Nova Scotia in February 1782, but a higher salary attracted him to Cape Breton as Chief Justice in 1784. Commission of Gibbons as Clerk of the Common Pleas, in PANS, Commission Book, CLXIV, 332; commission as Attorney General, in PANS, Documents, CCCXLVII, 42.

the contractor and the contractor's agent, etc. on a subject of little materiality."[20]

1785 drew to a close with DesBarres prepared to let neither his antagonisms nor his colonists die. Yorke had sent some correspondence back to headquarters in Halifax where General Campbell came to the conclusion that the governor was exceeding his powers. He told the colonel to keep the provisions and dole them out only to his troops, who were living in unfinished barracks and rotting tents, and those Loyalists (about forty, led by Cuyler) who recognized him as commanding officer. Yorke, who had supplies to last until June, was forced to admit that many other civilians would die if not helped by the military. In the meantime, DesBarres wrote directly to Campbell reminding him of his repeated assurances "that the necessary supply of provisions would be sent for the support of the settlers of this Government," and complaining that Storey's conduct was intolerable. On the island itself he tried to rally support with an address, which may well have been drafted by Gibbons, from the "merchants, traders, and other inhabitants of Sydney," praising him for his efforts on behalf of the colony.

DesBarres showed his weakness as an administrator, one of whose marks should be that he never issues an order he cannot back up with force, when he tried to compel Yorke to hand over the provisions obtained from the *Brandywine*. A physical fight between subordinates of the two men was only narrowly averted. The colonel offered to give up 40,000 rations, the exact amount of the consignment on the vessel, if the governor promised to replace them and pay the Treasury, but thereby he surrendered nothing of the disputed ground of authority on the island. If both sides had concentrated on the immediate problem of feeding all the settlers and the long-range problem of ensuring the island's future, if the economy could have been moved from barely above subsistence level, if DesBarres' belief that the general would shortly be replaced—had all these happened—reconciliation could have taken place. But nothing of the sort occurred during DesBarres' term.

20. In his letter of November 22 to DesBarres, Yorke had expressed surprise that DesBarres did not know better than to try to disobey the orders of a superior officer. It hardly justified the caustic tone of DesBarres' reply, DesBarres to Yorke, November 29, 1785, C. O. 217.

On the first day of 1786 the dispute, hitherto a local nuisance, became a matter of imperial interest. Campbell wrote to Lord Sydney, the Secretary of State, enclosing copies of much of the relevant correspondence and raising the whole issue of civil-military relations.[21] Naturally he offered an *ex parte* view, oblivious of the fact that the governor's claim came within a long British tradition upholding the supremacy of the civil authorities. Whitehall, which had failed to designate powers clearly, now had to decide important matters. Where did ultimate power lie? To whom were supplies consigned and who was responsible for their distribution?

Cape Breton, a minor cog in the imperial machinery, could not be given much ministerial time and the bureaucrats, as always, were shy about answering fundamental questions. The very news of the quarrel effectively determined the governor's fate. The island was too small and the role of the colony too tangential for it to be tolerated as a problem. By the time DesBarres recognized the furor and sent the chief justice to London, there was little chance of presenting a winning brief even though the lawyer was steadfast in his contention that "the civil powers of government are supreme over all manner of persons, civil, military, and ecclesiastical, of whatever rank, title or degree whatsoever" and "all military powers and authorities whatever . . . are in time of peace and within the British dominions amenable to the civil power and examinable, controulable and punishable in proper court of common law."[22]

Such a position was legally quite sound, but as an advocate Gibbons was pretentious and ineffective. Even had he been more persuasive, it is unlikely that DesBarres would have been totally exonerated. If there was not peace in and no profit from a colony, the natural presumption was to blame the chief official. Friends in England came to his aid too late and too weakly. In November 1786 Sydney decided to recall DesBarres, leaving the senior councilor in charge pending the governor's return to the island or the arrival of his replacement. The Secretary's decision was based principally on the informal, irregular manner in which the colony's finances had been handled and the disturbances which had occurred. He also castigated the "disposition . . .

21. Campbell to Sydney, January 27, 1786, C. O. 217.

22. Opinion of Chief Justice Gibbons, March 6, 1786, enclosed in Campbell to Sydney, March 15, 1787, C. O. 217.

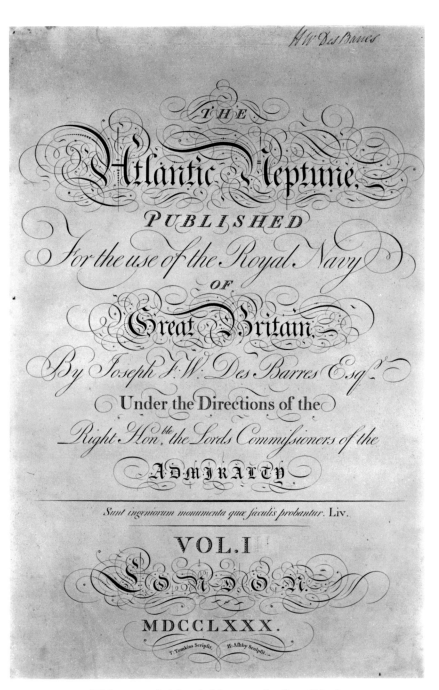

THE

Atlantic Neptune,

PUBLISHED

For the use of the Royal Navy

OF

Great Britain

By Joseph F. W. Des Barres Esqr.

Under the Directions of the

Right Honble. the Lords Commissioners of the

ADMIRALTY

Sunt ingeniorum monumenta quæ sæculis probantur. Liv.

VOL. I

LONDON.

MDCCLXXX.

T. Tomkins Scripsit. H. Ashby Sculpsit.

Title page of Atlantic Neptune (1780 edition).
Courtesy of Augustus P. Loring and The Peabody Museum.

View of the Sand Hills on the Isle of Sable, off the Nova Scotia coast.

Sketch of Wreckers Den on the Isle of Sable.

Courtesy of Augustus P. Loring and The Peabody Museum.

View of the Entrance of Louisbourg Harbor, Cape Breton Island.

Courtesy of Augustus P. Loring and The Peabody Museum.

View of Richmond Isle, near Gut of Canso, Nova Scotia.

Courtesy of Augustus P. Loring and The Peabody Museum.

View of Town and Harbor of Halifax from the Dartmouth shore.

Presumed to be DesBarres in comparative youth.
Courtesy of John J. Tufnell.

JOSEPH FREDERICK WALLET DES BARRES

Presumed to be DesBarres in later life.

Courtesy of John J. Tufnell.

to encourage a disunion of affection" between Cape Breton and Nova Scotia and concluded there was reason to doubt "the rectitude of your conduct, or at least of the prudence and discretion."

Criticism of DesBarres' relations with the military was deserved, although Yorke was by no means blameless. So also was the reprimand regarding his attitude toward Nova Scotia; where the future of Cape Breton was concerned, the governor had some megalomaniac tendencies. Inevitably, the colonial administrator and the imperial minister viewed the financial measures from different viewpoints and DesBarres' concern for the lives of the settlers was ignored in the criticism of his purchases of supplies. The "considerable expense . . . unnecessarily incurred" was the home government's primary concern, but the governor did not view matters in quite the same light. In April 1787 he was informed that Lieut. Colonel Macarmick, who had been appointed to "act as Lieut. Governor of the Island of Cape Breton during your absence," would shortly sail to the island, but DesBarres made no effort to hurry home and stayed in Cape Breton until October.[23] One of his last actions was to obtain a license to occupy a tract of Crown land, a nice symbol of his faith both in himself and the island's future.

Many of DesBarres' programs were well conceived. His plans to develop the island's coal deposits were essentially sound, although in the eyes of the British government they were further examples of the governor's propensity for moving beyond his Instructions. After the American Revolution the policy of keeping these mines strictly for Crown use and profit was clearly restated.[24] Yet when Admiral Camp-

23. Sydney to DesBarres, April 5, 1787, C. O. 217. The exact words of the statement are important because DesBarres was later to make a claim for half salary during his absence, on the grounds that he had been temporarily recalled, not relieved of his office. See Chapter V. By additional Instructions sent out in December 1786, Sydney had revoked DesBarres' power of nominating the Council, appointing its members directly. Mathews, Moncrieff, Smith, and Bousseau were among those who regained both their seats and an opportunity to oppose DesBarres' measures.

24. For Cape Breton supplies of coal to the British forces see Lord North to Sir William Howe, June 25, 1776, American Headquarters Papers (PAC transcripts), IV, 133, General Howe to General Massey, September 3, 1776, ibid., XXIX, 93, Memorial of William Russell to Massey, October 1778, ibid., XVI, 166; Captain Phips to General Haldimand, July 26, 1781, Haldimand Papers (PAC transcripts), CXL, 168 and Major Mathews to Major Nairne, August 20, 1781, ibid., CXL, 110. The coal was again of value during Britain's next war. See, for example, General George Prevost to General Sir James Craig, May 9, 1808, Commanding Royal Engineers Correspondence (PAC transcripts), CCXXVI, 52. The case of the civilians was put in a petition from the Nova Scotia House of Assembly

bell in Newfoundland reported "considerable saving will arise by having supplies of coals from time to time from the island of Cape Breton," permission was given for Newfoundlanders to dig and carry out the required amounts. In contrast, there was no encouragement for the governor's attempts to work the mines which constituted one of his island's principal assets. There was similar disapproval of DesBarres' ambitious ideas for attracting settlers. Realizing that the location, climate, and youth of the colony militated against extensive immigration and that even at the Loyalist exodus no great numbers came, the governor was correct in his belief that vigorous recruitment was necessary. Unfortunately good plans became entwined in the island's political controversies. As a result, it is almost impossible to judge the effectiveness of DesBarres' efforts. Population estimates—and we have no solid census figures for any year between 1774 and 1811—reflect the position of the protagonists in the civil-military dispute. Yorke, Cuyler and their supporters kept figures down, in an attempt to limit rations and discredit DesBarres. He and his adherents claimed steady increases in numbers and stressed the improvements which were taking place, to try to impress the officials at home.[25] Another source of trouble was DesBarres' sympathy with the Acadian inhabitants and his recognition of their value, a position not in harmony with the feelings of the authorities in London.

Even more indicative of the divergence in views is the policy toward prospective American immigrants. The island was not paradise but neither was it a place without hope, and DesBarres was by no means alone in his optimism. Cuyler had obviously thought Cape Breton had possibilities and another interested observer, William Smith, saw a future for it as a nursery for British seamen and an entrepôt in the triangular trade of Great Britain, North America, and the West Indies. It would also provide an admirable base when "necessity calls for it" to "destroy the American trade and make depredations *ad libitum* along their coast."[26] Although Smith was opposed to any-

---

to the King, November 27, 1755, Dartmouth Papers (Originals), II, 1214. Another view may be found in the journal of Captain William Owen, published in the *Bulletin* of the New York Public Library, XXXV (February 1931).

25. DesBarres' estimate that when he left the island the population was over 4,000 is undoubtedly inaccurate.

26. William Smith to Shelburne, April 28, 1785, Shelburne Papers (PAC transcripts), LXXXVIII, 73. Smith's views were further developed in *A Caveat against Emigration to*

thing connected with the late American colonies, even the Loyalists whom he described as "a set of mercenary contractors and unprincipled people," the governor did not share this prejudice and in September 1785 issued a proclamation inviting American refugees to the colony.[27] When Thomas Venture was sent to the American states in search of provisions he made some efforts to encourage migration to Cape Breton as well.[28] From Whitehall came censure for the governor's attempts to entice Americans away from Nantucket and Martha's Vineyard, although later the home government was happy to resettle them in Wales. On the rock of expenditure all DesBarres' schemes foundered, including an immigration plan which had much merit.[29]

In the Maritimes a legend has grown up of DesBarres as a rapacious governor. His highhanded manner and his less than winsome personality helped its creation. But history is, of course, more complicated than fable. Balancing official documents and private papers, seeking evidence from both sides of the controversies, reinvestigating the charges of dishonesty, the historian has to declare that the worst possible verdict is "not proven." On the question of his responsibility for the failure of the colony to prosper, it is just as clear that placing the blame entirely on the governor's shoulders is much too simple. The causes may be more appropriately sought in a variety of elements, not least in the weaknesses in imperial policies.

The American Revolution hardly provided the shock necessary to produce deep changes in British imperialism.[30] In Cape Breton, and

---

America (London, 1803) in which he endeavored to cover every matter which could interest a prospective emigrant, including the fact that "The American ladies in general are pale, lifeless, indolent and pale of dress. At the age of twenty-five they have not so good constitutions as an English woman at the age of forty."

27. Proclamation dated September 1, 1785 in C. O. 217.

28. John Drummond, apparently sent on a similar mission from Newfoundland, met DesBarres' emissary at Newport, R. I. Later he said that in response to the governor's proclamation about 50 families from Connecticut and Rhode Island wanted to move. Examination of Drummond, December 20, 1785, C. O. 217. See also the deposition of James Angell, who sold a vessel to Venture, and other documents of the transactions filed together under this date.

29. In 1802, DesBarres drew up a succinct, optimistic but solid assessment of Cape Breton's advantages. See DesBarres Papers, Series V, p. 693. Although the paper is not dated, internal evidence makes clear when it was written; there is no reason to believe that the governor had changed his opinion substantially in the fifteen years since his recall.

30. Helen T. Manning, *British Colonial Government after the American Revolution* ("Yale Historical Publications, Miscellany," XXVI, New Haven, 1933), p. 14 sees the period 1782 to 1820 as one where the "spirit of political lethargy" brooded over the

in Nova Scotia also for that matter, the years immediately following the loss of the Thirteen Colonies saw no significant modifications of the old ideas and the old ways. If it is argued that the island was a small colony of no great importance, this is hardly true of Nova Scotia. Yet the pre-Revolutionary policy of restrictions designed to protect British interests, if necessary at the expense of the colonials, was continued. In the case of Cape Breton Whitehall's ignorance was glaringly obvious, together with failure to recognize local aspirations, realize and develop the colony's resources, and clarify the distribution of power. Such characteristics may sound more typical of the 1760's, but so far as the island was concerned they were still very apparent two decades and a revolution later.

Ironically, it was a mistake to send DesBarres to Cape Breton at all. Whatever his talents they were not those best suited to handling the problems of a young and neglected colony. Tact, a spirit of compromise, the ability to encourage others, a flair for conveying his vision of a prosperous Cape Breton, were not his strongest qualities. Personal insecurities made him appear egotistical and his actions arrogant. He lacked the backing of the few men who had some administrative experience although at least one of these, Abraham Cuyler, was from the beginning so proud and so jealous that he could have never given the governor his full support. Soon after Macarmick arrived he restored Cuyler to all his offices, but before long he too quarreled with the eager subordinate who finally resigned and quit the island. Cape Breton's opportunity to develop as a semi-independent colony was by no means the open door it had once seemed. The colony was severely hampered by the narrowly conceived policies of the Mother Country and its unwillingness to allow local officials to exercise discretion in the development of local resources. Such limitations were all the more galling to a man of DesBarres' romantic temperament and the venting of his frustrations helped to embitter relations between him and other stubborn, ambitious men.

---

colonies. Vincent T. Harlow, *The Founding of the Second British Empire, 1763-1793* (London, 1952) plays down the effect of the Revolution on British imperial policies and so does Peter Marshall, "The British Empire and the American Revolution," *Huntington Library Quarterly*, XXVII (February 1964), 135-45 and "The First and Second British Empires," *History*, XLIX (1964), 13-23.

CHAPTER V

Probity and Policies

WAS DesBarres honest while in public service? The question was not fully answered by his contemporary investigators and perhaps cannot finally be determined by his historian, but there is no lack of material on which to base some conclusions. British officials pored over hundreds of pages of public accounts, keenly scrutinized his private financial records, and perused long-winded and laudatory claims for more than four decades. The second appointment as a governor, in 1804, may be regarded as a vindication of his honor, but DesBarres rightly felt that the imperial government gave him neither compensation matching his claims nor any clear exoneration despite the opinion of those who actually examined his accounts that there was no basis for charging him with malfeasance.

He was suspected of irregularities in connection with two of his major services under British governments, the nautical surveys leading to publication of the *Atlantic Neptune* and his administration in Cape Breton. The two were linked by more than the fact that in his later statements he lumped together his claims in each area. Failure to resolve fully the questions springing from the hydrographical expenses played a direct part in his appointment to Cape Breton. In both cases, the expenditures which Whitehall declared excessive partly resulted from ambiguities in the terms of appointment. In executing each task DesBarres found that the funds given him were not enough for the level of performance he wanted, but he made matters worse with an accounting system which was not sufficiently specific and orderly.

Since no complete analysis of his capital can be given it would be foolish to state categorically that DesBarres did not personally benefit from his public careers, especially since this was the accepted practice in the eighteenth century. But at least three things point to the validity of his claims. His declaration that the expenses of his surveys were much less than those of his contemporaries, such as Holland and De-Brahm, was never seriously contested. His most important purchases of real estate occurred in the decade before his return to England or were made very shortly afterwards, that is before he had access to the large sums involved in making the *Neptune*. The period over which there was the greatest dispute, namely 1773 to 1787, coincided with a decrease rather than an increase in his personal resources. Together, these facts add up to impressive circumstantial evidence.

In his hydrographic work DesBarres, under poorly defined conditions, lacked both adequate capital and personnel.[1] He proceeded on the assumption that he could not be expected to carry on the work alone, that he was relatively free to hire those who had qualifications valuable to the project, and that reimbursement would come in due course. This rather naive attitude was not in keeping with the one held by the bureaucrats who served the parsimonious British government. Yet various factors made DesBarres hopeful. He saw that the land surveys in North America were well financed and expected the coastal ones would in time be similarly supported. After his return to London in 1773 the outbreak of the American Revolution led to signally increased requests for copies of his charts and the resulting commission to engrave and publish them in large quantities encouraged him to think the administration recognized that in wartime their value exceeded that of the land surveys. Even after the loss of the Thirteen Colonies the usefulness of charts which delineated the dangers to shipping in North American waters with far more accuracy than any of their predecessors could surely be considered greater than surveys of lands which were mostly no longer in the empire. DesBarres' repeated claims may have been both irritating and contentious but they did represent unpaid costs of important contributions to British mercantile and naval power.

From the story of his long, complex, repetitive, and confusing correspondence with various individuals and government departments may be deduced his guilt or innocence on the charge of fraud, the charge which in a nice way was thrown at him repeatedly. During his first years as an Admiralty surveyor he was careful to inform the naval authorities in American waters of the nature and progress of his work. These reports were passed on to Whitehall, which commended him

1. Lord Colville, who was not empowered to defray any expenses except the hire of vessels, even suggested that DesBarres would not care to undertake the work on the vague terms offered him. Lords of the Admiralty to Colville, December 8, 1764, DesBarres Papers, Series V, p. 34 and Lords of the Admiralty to the King, July 12, 1781, Privy Council 1/57; copy in DesBarres Papers, Series III, p. 22.

for his efforts.[2] The question was whether it would continue to do so once it realized not just the value of the charts but also the time and money involved. Commodore Hood, Colville's successor as naval commander in North America, was very sympathetic to DesBarres' plans, but in 1767 he inadvertently opened the first round in the long fight between hydrographer and government by declaring he did not feel empowered to meet the costs without specific authorization from home.[3] Almost certainly the amount, a mere £600, was not at issue. But the terms of service had been left unclear, and the position of an army officer serving naval masters was more than a little equivocal. Not for the first time did a man find that crossing service lines was a step fraught with peril!

When he sent the accounts on to London, Hood said that if the intention had been to pay the costs of DesBarres' instruments and his contingent expenses then his case was entirely just. This is a point worthy of special attention. Despite his unwillingness to pay the bills without consultation, Hood did not in any way raise the question of whether they had been padded. He was simply concerned with the precise terms of DesBarres' commission and with discovering whether the Admiralty would accept full responsibility for all the costs. The Admiralty said it would not, offering the lame excuse that "although they had in their letter to Lord Colville encouraged Mr. DesBarres to expect an allowance for instruments and contingent expenses they did not imagine that he would proceed to such a length as he had done."[4] This news did not reach the surveyor until June 1770 and for two more summers at least he carried on much as before in the hope that "when the work should be completed their Lordships would be so satisfied with its importance and the necessity of the charges attendant thereupon that no further objection would be made to them."[5]

Such an attitude was a nice blend of ingenuousness and dedication. It was also, in a way, quite practical. A second specific request would

2. Philip Stephens to DesBarres, June 12, 1767, DesBarres Papers, Series V, p. 46.

3. Stephens' reply to Hood, dated December 9, 1769, is noted in DesBarres to Stephens, May 8, 1779, ibid., p. 179.

4. Reported in Lord Commissioners of the Admiralty to the King, July 12, 1781, Privy Council 1/57, Bundle marked "Colonial, 1782"; copy in DesBarres Papers, Series III, p. 22.

5. Observations of DesBarres on report from the Admiralty, July 12, 1781, DesBarres Papers, Series V, p. 285. They were written between July and December, 1781.

probably take another three years to answer. In the meantime, much more of the Nova Scotia coast could be charted. If he waited for a reply, what should he do in the interim? Wasn't the government more likely to honor his bills when he could present a large and completed work? Could he reduce costs and realistically expect to produce anything of value? Thinking along these lines, DesBarres had no choice. He went on with the chart making and the expenses did not decrease. It is hard to see that they could have done. Previous claims were to cover such necessary items as buying instruments and paper, hiring a shallop, paying house rent, and providing fuel. DesBarres also found it difficult to believe that his charges were excessive when they averaged just a little more than £150 a year, and Holland had "a fine supply of astronomical instruments and also £800 per annum to pay his assistants plus extraordinary expenses independent of his salary and the fees of his office."[6]

Although he went back to England in 1773, he allowed six years to go by before presenting a petition concerning the costs of his surveys. His explanation was that he first wanted his work to win "the most effectual testimonies of my diligence and of the value of my long and faithful services, confirmed by the unanimous and distinguished approbation of all judicious navigators who have examined and had opportunity to experience the accuracy of my charts."[7] Of course these were the very busy years in which both the first and second editions of the *Neptune* were made. It was one of the happiest periods in his life. He was at home in London with friends who offered company and instilled him with confidence while he was directing a staff larger than he had ever had before and bringing to fruition the labors of his many years of surveying. There was another spur to achievement in the possibility that the Admiralty would finally establish a hydrographic section and appoint him as its head.[8]

6. DesBarres to Hood, August 13, 1770, ibid., p. 56, written after he had met Holland at Liverpool, N. S., and discussed with him their respective surveys. The office to which DesBarres referred was that of Surveyor General of the Province of Quebec. See Willis Chipman, "The Life and Times of Major Samuel Holland," *Papers and Records*, Ontario Hist. Soc., XXI (1924), 43. An example of the detailed comparison between DesBarres' and Holland's accounts may be found in DesBarres Papers, Series III, p. 45.

7. DesBarres to Stephens, May 8, 1779, DesBarres Papers, Series V, p. 179.

8. DesBarres to Lord of Commissioners of the Treasury, January 28, 1794, Treasury Board, Registered Papers, T1/372; copy in DesBarres Papers, Series III, p. 6, and Howe to DesBarres, April 26, 1782, DesBarres Papers, Series V, p. 331.

Relations with the government department were still confused and the payment for the years 1763-1774 left unresolved. Even the production of the *Neptune* was hindered by lack of money, just as the surveys had been, and once again the contract terms were not precise. The ambiguity did not apparently worry DesBarres at the time but it bedeviled his claims later.[9] In 1779 he presented another petition concerning his survey expenses. When the Royal Navy was using his charts in its war against the rebellious Americans and their French ally DesBarres was trying to get what he thought was his due. At the end of the war, when the British government was strapped for money and swamped with a variety of importuning merchants, Loyalists, and military men, it granted nearly all of his claims and made him lieutenant governor of Cape Breton, partly in recognition of the fact that his professions and persistence had been justified.

Tracing the course of DesBarres' petitions from 1779 to their acceptance offers insights into the ways of British bureaucracy in the last part of the eighteenth century. His memorial of 1779 to the Privy Council was passed on to the Admiralty in March 1781 and a report sent back to the council in July.[10] His claims can be examined under five headings. With regard to surveying and astronomical instruments, drawing tools and paper, the Admiralty suggested that although not all were necessary he should be repaid for their costs once he handed over the instruments.[11] It was recognized that most of them had been obtained before the Admiralty's resolution of 1769 and that they would be extremely useful in any future surveys. Secondly, there were the expenses arising from the employment of assistants, pilots, and guides at a rate of half a guinea a day, which in ten years had totaled nearly £2,000. No claim had been submitted during the first four years "nor was it imagined that such a claim would be made," and their Lordships' advice was that nothing be paid "more especially

9. Samuel Holland thought of DesBarres as being "indifferent in his finances." See Holland to Haldimand, March 16, 1773, Haldimand Collection, PANS.

10. A copy of the memorial with the report of the Admiralty is in DesBarres Papers, Series V, pp. 274-78, 280-84.

11. Complete details of the instruments used by DesBarres are not available. The Navy Office requested the return of a sextant, telescope, astronomical quadrant, another with reflecting telescope, a pair of 17-inch globes, and a pair of beam compasses. See Commissioners of the Navy to DesBarres, December 26, 1783, ibid., p. 355. The globes cost 3 gns. each, the astronomical quadrant £60, and the reflecting telescope £40, according to DesBarres. See his reply December 29, 1783, ibid., p. 357.

as we find that the persons who assisted Mr. DesBarres in this work were borne for wages and victuals the time they were employed."

The third claim, for the wages of an instrument maker and repairer at £40 per year from May 1, 1766, was also rejected. The Admiralty believed employment of such a person on an annual basis was unnecessary and pointedly remarked that DesBarres should have terminated his services as soon as he received the earlier resolution on expenses. Fourthly, there was a claim of £80 per annum to cover the costs of house rent and fuel. In recommending that nothing be paid, the Board explained that in the accounts presented for the period up to September 30, 1767, the charge was only £50 each year and even this had previously been disallowed. Lastly, DesBarres claimed for deficiencies in the provisions supplied for the crews and for losses sustained in boats sunk, overturned, or stolen by Indians. The sum requested averaged £60 per annum. On the grounds that "it is natural to suppose that considerable quantities of provisions were lost or damaged in the manner specified in the account," it was agreed that he would be paid, providing he delivered "such vouchers for the payment of the money as he shall be able to produce or in failure thereof verifying the payment upon oath."

DesBarres received eminently fair treatment under the first and last headings but the Board's negative reaction to the ones in between left him some £3,600 short of his stated expenses. An additional request for compensation for loss of rank and emoluments in his profession, the result of spending fifteen years working on the surveys and charts, was tactfully brushed aside. His reactions to the report were vigorous, and in a second memorial to the King in Council he presented his observations.[12] After declaring that he was quite prepared to deliver the instruments to any designated person, he accounted for their cost in greater detail.[13] On the question of assistants he showed up the amphibology under which he had worked, without fully demonstrating the creditability of his contention. He explained that he had held himself responsible for his assistants, adding that although they might be down in the books as having received wages and victuals from the

12. Memorial of DesBarres to the King in Council, 1782, DesBarres Papers, Series III, p. 36.

13. DesBarres by the time of this memorial had received £132.10s.0d., exactly the sum of his costs in 1764. This left £592.10s.0d. outstanding, his annual expenses under this item having ranged from £12.10s.7d. (1773) to £270.16s.8d. (1767).

Navy they constantly ate at his table. The average cost was thirteen shillings and sixpence a day. Allowances should be made for the situation of an isolated army officer dependent upon naval supplies and arrangements, but the item remains a weak part in his case.

In stressing the need for an instrument repairer, DesBarres noted the stormy conditions under which he and his assistants worked, and in explaining the bill for rent and fuel he showed how during the winter months the charts were formed and improved on the basis of the data obtained in the summer. These were specific and sound answers but he could not forebear from introducing a note of personal grievance, contending that, if he had not engaged in the chart making, he would have become a lieutenant colonel instead of being merely a captain.

Later in 1782 he wrote another memorial for the Privy Council which in form and spirit anticipated many others yet to come. Following the standard practice of his times, he began with a narrative of all his service under the Crown and then made advantageous comparisons between his work and its results and the surveys of Holland and DeBrahm. DesBarres believed his were all the more creditable because of the large financial support they had received. In October the Admiralty sent a second report to the Council in reply to its request for a reconsideration of the first and DesBarres' forceful observations. The recommendations were now very favorable, possibly but not necessarily a reflection of the appointment of Admiral Augustine Keppel as First Lord of the Admiralty when the second Rockingham ministry was formed in the spring.[14] The sum claimed for instruments was to be totally paid on their delivery. Even more gratifying was acceptance of his full claim for assistants, pilots and guides, and the expenses of an instrument maker. The need for such a person was now recognized, together with DesBarres' statement that the Board's resolutions had not been received until after the surveys had been in operation for six years. Five-eighths of the £800 for rent and fuel were granted. On the "losses in his profession" a naval board naturally was unable to help, but it added the statement that he was "deserving of

14. Keppel, who had been created a viscount on his appointment as First Lord, continued to hold his position when the Rockingham ministry gave way to the Shelburne administration in July 1782. He was replaced by Richard, Viscount Howe in January 1783, regained the post in April 1783, and gave it up again to Howe in December 1783. Howe then held it until July 1788, when he was succeeded by the Earl of Chatham.

some mark of His Majesty's favor as a further reward for his zeal, activity and ability in presenting and completing the above mentioned useful work." The Council also accepted all he asked for goods lost or stolen.[15] In short, the reports amounted to a vindication of DesBarres' honesty and a recognition of the value of his work. On only one count had he received less than he sought and even there the justice of a claim had been accepted.[16]

His integrity might have been upheld but DesBarres continued to believe he was unjustifiably out-of-pocket. Another memorial, dated the first of May 1784, emphasized the financial difficulties into which he had been driven because his salary and expenditures had not been promptly paid. Although most of his expenses from the years 1764 to 1773 were now to be met, he had no compensation "for the expence he has been at in the advance of the aforementioned disbursements during so many years." According to him the cumulative interest, to December 1783, came to nearly £6,000. In addition, the costs of publishing the charts since 1774, about £5,475, were unpaid as was his stipend between the end of August 1770 and the end of June 1784. There was little chance he would get back his interest money but the request for salary and expenses was more likely to be awarded, especially since his survey bills had been allowed.

Acceptance of the surveying costs was an indirect and partial validation of the *Neptune* charges. But this was not the only reason for his placing them in the later series of petitions. The attempts to obtain the costs of publication blossomed only when it did not appear that the sales of the charts would cover them. By cause and character they were linked to those of his surveys, although three years of administration in Cape Breton divided the Privy Council's allowance of the survey claim and DesBarres' full scale submission of his publication costs. Then they were contained in statements covering his Cape Breton tenure as well as his hydrographic work. It is therefore appropriate to examine the *Neptune* outlays separately for the period before 1784, and thereafter as part of DesBarres' total demands.

The starting point should be the terms of employment, which employer and employee again viewed differently. DesBarres remained

15. Report of the Lords of the Privy Council, November 1783, Privy Council 1/57; copy in DesBarres Papers, Series III, p. 67.

16. Report of the Lords of the Admiralty to a committee of His Majesty's Privy Council, October 21, 1782, ibid., p. 58.

a servant of the Crown but his position as an army officer with two other masters, the Admiralty and the Board of Trade, allowed him to enter into something akin to a contract with the British government. In May 1775 the Admiralty decided that the expense involved in engraving and printing the charts of the coasts of Ireland made by Murdoch Mackenzie and those by DesBarres of the Atlantic coast of North America was so great, £2,000 and £4,000 respectively, that parliamentary approval was needed.[17] While it was being sought, DesBarres received an allowance of twenty shillings a day and a grant of ten guineas a year for stationery and supplies. This was continued until August 1779, some six years after he completed his survey work. He was also given to understand that any profits from the sale of his charts would go into his own pocket. In some respects, he was simply an army officer at the call of naval superiors; in others he was in the same situation as the private chart makers of his day.[18]

The outbreak of the American Revolution affected DesBarres' activities in a variety of ways. It led to an immediate call for the charts and opened the possibility of a large market before the financial agreement with the government had been fully discussed. His belief that the accuracy and detail of his charts would win rapid recognition and lead to a handsome profit was buttressed, but the ravaging of his estates by American privateers deprived him of important mortgage capital when he badly needed it. He was therefore in a very perplexing financial predicament. With costs far from covered, without any firm assurance of any official or unofficial sales, except by sacrificing his right to the profit, and under constant pressure to produce the charts with the minimum of delay, he was hardly in a position to bargain with the Admiralty. In these circumstances, the outstanding quality of the *Neptune* is little short of a miracle.

DesBarres expected that, despite the subsidy, he could personally sell the charts; apparently he thought of himself as a semi-independent entrepreneur and the Navy as the principal subscriber to his work. Curious as this may seem, it was implicitly accepted by the Admiralty. For example, it was ordered that he should be paid an

17. Resolution of the Lords of the Admiralty regarding memorial of Mr. DesBarres, Admiralty Sec., Minutes Ad. 3/80; copy in ibid., p. 1.

18. On the private chart makers see Adrian H. W. Robinson, *Marine Cartography in Britain* (Leicester, England, 1962), pp. 84, 114.

amount of £264.5s.0d. for charts sent to Howe.[19] The admiral had received 36 sets of charts of Nova Scotia, each containing 72 plates, and 36 sets of charts of New England, each containing 41 plates. The charge was one shilling per plate, but the cost of binding each volume was far greater. DesBarres was also in the habit of sending complimentary copies of his work to influential people, such as the dukes of Cumberland and York.[20] He told Howe that he was dispatching charts to him "on my own risque and account," and added that he had "run myself deeply into debt to perform the beneficial public duty your Lordship did me the honor to entrust to my care as a faithful servant to the Crown and Public."[21] Here lay the crux of the matter, whom was DesBarres serving—the Crown or his own coffers, the public or his own pocket?

In 1794, in one of the most complete presentations of his accounts and claims, DesBarres made a statement of what had been allowed him by the British government with respect to the *Neptune*. Between 1774 and 1784 he had been granted £3,711.15s.0d. by the 1775 vote of the Commons, £2,000 by a vote of 1777, £1,885 in 1778, £1,450 in 1779, and £1,486.15s.0d. in 1780. On each of these votes he made a deduction for fees, which averaged about 8 percent. He had also received pay at the rate of twenty shillings a day from January 1764 to August 1779, a total of £5,722. Against these receipts he placed his expenses between 1764 and 1784, and included a demand for "indemnification for losses sustained in the necessary advance of money for carrying on the above mentioned services." The sum owed him was over £15,000 of which the claim for survey work was £300 and the claim for publication expenses more than eleven times this. The remainder was money pledged in Cape Breton and interest on the total amount.[22]

One person at least felt he was more private chart maker than public

19. Lords of the Admiralty to the Navy Boards, September 13, 1776, Admiralty Secretary, Out Letters, Lords Letters, 1776, Admiralty 2/244; copy in DesBarres Papers, Series III, p. 2. See also DesBarres to Stephens, July 24, 1779, enclosing accounts of charts supplied and Stephens to DesBarres, August 4, 1779, DesBarres Papers, Series V, pp. 188, 191. The *Atlantic Neptune*, in the stage reached at this date, cost seven guineas.

20. James Luttrell to DesBarres, February 1, 1773, ibid., p. 87.

21. DesBarres also told Philip Stephens that Howe had led him to understand that "the Admiralty should take at least 100 setts of my work which were to be supplied to the King's Ships in America and charged in like manner as naval stores." DesBarres to Stephens, February 27, 1777, DesBarres Papers, Series V, p. 162.

22. DesBarres to Lord Commissioners of the Treasury, January 28, 1794, Treasury Board, Registered Papers, T1/732; copy in DesBarres Papers, Series III, pp. 7, 8.

employee. The widow of a Nova Scotia governor wrote him to ask for a map of Rhode Island and Providence because she understood that he "distributes to his friends."[23] There is also evidence that the Treasury, on the recommendation of the Board of Trade, paid him 35 guineas a plate, and this later became a key point in the ministry's argument that both his salary and expenses had been met. Its position was that he was a public servant who had been permitted a large amount of individual initiative on a special assignment. By 1778 DesBarres was receiving almost three quarters of the money allowed by Parliament in connection with the surveys in North America. It was hoped the *Neptune* would be finished that year but it was not until the next that he could say "the completion of these 26 plates, which will be effected in the course of this year, will bring the whole undertaking to a conclusion."[24] When he again left England in 1784 his survey expenses had all been paid, but the engraving and publication costs remained outstanding. On his return three years later the situation had changed considerably. The British government had been hard pressed financially by the inevitable postwar debts. The hydrographer had proved to be an embarrassing governor, whose probity was again in question and whose debts were now greater than ever.

In addition to the various economic and political problems he encountered as governor of Cape Breton DesBarres, who in his buoyancy had accepted the inflated estimates of the island's worth made earlier in the century by people as informed as Edmund Burke, was hampered by a creaky imperial apparatus.[25] He commenced his administration by sending his accounts to London promptly and regularly. When these

23. Lady William Campbell to DesBarres, February 1777, DesBarres Papers, Series V, p. 151. Replies from various other people who thanked DesBarres for sending copies of one or more items in the *Atlantic Neptune* may be found in ibid., pp. 200-73.

24. Plantations General, 1766-1780 North America, Estimate of the Expense attending General Surveys of His Majesty's Dominions in North America, 1779, C. O. 324, XVIII; copy in DesBarres Papers, Series III, p. 161.

25. Examples are John Oldmixon, *The British Empire in America* (2d ed. rev.; 2 vols.; London, 1741), I, 237. The first edition appeared in 1708. William Bollan, *The Importance and Advantage of Cape Breton, Truly Stated and Impartially Considered* (London, 1746), p. 73. This work should not be confused with the anonymous *The Importance of Cape Breton Consider'd; in a Letter to a Member of Parliament, from an Inhabitant of New England*, which was also published in London in 1746. Edmund Burke placed special emphasis on the advantages of Louisbourg in colonial trade, concluding that Cape Breton though a small settlement was "perhaps of more consequence than all the rest" of French Canada. *An Account of the European Settlements in America* (2d ed. rev.; 2 vols.; London, 1758-60), II, 33. The first edition appeared in 1757.

bills were paid he assumed that his policies were approved. Optimistic as always, he expected that "prodigious numbers on the coast of the American states" wished to emigrate and to prepare for their reception drew up a model town-plan for Sydney. He also created a new accounting system which in his long-winded fashion he described as "a method appearing conducive to perspecuity for reimbursing all manner of occasionally necessary expenditures, which was to draw bills on my personal agent in favor of those who made the supplies and to transmit quarterly accounts to office for the part of the expence chargeable to the public." On the ill-founded assumption of the colony's agent he drew three thousand pounds on the Treasury to balance what he already advanced in the anticipation that "my Bills would be honored."[26] This was not a sound judgment either of the agent's report or the ways of Whitehall, and DesBarres only made matters worse for himself through his tendency to form grandiose dreams and then believe they had come true. His statement that by September 1785 he had to care for between three and four thousand people is undoubtedly an exaggeration. Even with the influx of Loyalists the colony's population had not tripled in eleven years. His declaration that in the first two years of his administration the island exported goods worth more than forty thousand pounds and that in five years this figure would have increased fivefold is also not acceptable as the whole truth.[27] What is more credible is DesBarres' stake in the progress of the colony, and the "inundation of bills, damages, and expenses" which he met from his own resources, the pledging of the *Neptune's* plates, and the mortgaging of his estates. In considerable measure the necessity for such actions arose from the relatively primitive stage of the economy, the need for heavy expenditures, and the absence of any legislature with power to vote money in the customary way combined with an express prohibition, in the governor's commission, against levying taxes.[28]

26. The important matter of DesBarres' financial methods is discussed in Audit Office, 3/142, Cape Breton, 1784-1801, Governor's Accounts; copy in DesBarres Papers, Series III, p. 143, in DesBarres to Sir Wm. Dolben, Sir Herbert Mackworth, and George Bambridge, May 13, 1790, DesBarres Papers, Series V, pp. 1137-82, especially p. 1167, n. 1, and in draft of report of William Baldwin, 1798/99, ibid., 2264.

27. DesBarres Papers, Series III, p. 140. Cuyler had entertained similarly large hopes for the island. See Cuyler to Nepean, April 3, 1784, C. O. 217.

28. The civil list totaled £2,550 in 1785, Nepean to DesBarres, July 28, 1785, DesBarres Papers, Series V, p. 813. It was £1,840 in 1801, and by 1816 had only risen to

DesBarres was also involved in personal investment in Cape Breton. Indeed he would have been less than human, in eighteenth century terms, if private concerns had not been linked with public officeholding. Of course the success of his ventures would also aid the colony and bring credit to his governorship. The agent for his enterprise was the Acadia Company, formed about 1775 for the purpose of obtaining lands in Nova Scotia and settling emigrants on them. DesBarres held nearly a third of the total shares, and among his partners two of the most distinguished were Admiral Robert Digby and William Windham, later secretary at war.[29] The American Revolution made the company postpone its plans but after the peace a search for prospective tenants was begun, with DesBarres' appointment making Cape Breton a more attractive proposition than mainland Nova Scotia. Although eighty willing families were found the Acadia company, like so many other enterprises in which DesBarres was involved, was poorly managed and its Irish agent, George Rutherford, had to cancel the orders for supplies and the hiring of a vessel. Even if the company had prospered, it is questionable whether an increase in settlers was Cape Breton's primary need in view of the difficulties experienced in feeding those already there. The governor may have been correct in thinking that one of his principal duties was to attract colonists, but the connection between private investor and public official, common as it was at the time, hardly accords with the injured innocence and bitter denunciations of his later memorials. He was right in charging that if he had received the promised support from Lord Sydney it would not have been necessary to recall him. There may be poignancy in his failure, but the harsh facts in the Acadia Company records show DesBarres as a land speculator who gambled, and lost.

At the close of 1785, so the governor claimed, he had advanced more than £11,000 and by the end of his administration this sum had doubled. Nearly £5,000 was spent on provisions, slightly more than £4,000 for materials for shelter for Loyalists and for public buildings, over £5,000 for wages, and over £3,000 for "contingencies," ranging from working oxen to bringing witnesses to England to support his

---

£2,194. See PANS, CCCXXXIII, Documents 77, 83. See also Helen T. Manning, *British Colonial Government after the American Revolution* ("Yale Historical Publications, Miscellany," XXVI, New Haven, 1933), pp. 57, 66, 193.

29. DesBarres Papers, Series V, p. 3047.

case.[30] His accounts were very specifically itemized. For some there are both declarations and explanations by persons other than Des-Barres.[31] Probably they are as honest as anyone could expect them to be under the system of patronage government then prevalent. Possibly the governor was trying to utilize his administrative office to recoup losses sustained in the *Atlantic Neptune* project and to find new capital to prop up his crumbling estates. It may be that he believed himself to be scrupulous but his delusions of grandeur drove him into a twilight zone where he was unable to distinguish between truth and falsehood, wish and fulfillment. Undoubtedly, he was the victim of maladministration, not only his own, but also that of an imperial government which inadequately financed the establishment of an independent colony in Cape Breton.

Each of these possibilities may contain an element of the whole truth, and they can act as guides in the murky meanderings of Des-Barres' financial affairs. Late in 1787 the governor sailed to the isle of Jersey. England, as he declared, was perilous because the secretary of state had not granted him a safe conduct and his creditors were eagerly waiting to throw him in jail. He had to take "a circuit in disguise, and after some hairbreadth escapes," arrived in London in April 1788. There he lodged in "one of those houses below Charing Cross which are kept for the accommodation of men in such unhappy circumstances," trying to live on his captain's pay of seven shillings and sixpence a day, almost constantly fending off the harrying creditors and trudging wearily through the warrens of Whitehall.

After problems with the survey accounts, the *Neptune* costs, and now administrative expenses, the Treasury officials naturally were a little suspicious. They demanded an explanation for every farthing spent. DesBarres was ordered to provide plans and estimates of the buildings "as if there had been insinuation that none had existed," which was precisely what Cuyler and Mathews had suggested. Complications arose because some of the vouchers sent from Cape Breton were lost between various government offices, and Under Secretary

---

30. DesBarres to Dundas, February 15, 1793, DesBarres Papers, Series III, p. 173.

31. The detailed character of the accounts is significant. They may be seen, together with the declarations and explanations, in DesBarres Papers, Series V, Vol. 7. Itemized financial records as well as fully documented assertions fill the bulk of *A Statement Submitted by Lieutenant Colonel Desbarres, for Consideration* (London, 1795), hereafter cited as DesBarres *Statement*. Copies in Rare Book Room, New York Public Library and PANS.

Nepean had to permit him to complete a new set from the triplicate copies in DesBarres' possession.[32] When Sydney retired from the Colonial office in June 1789 the case had only just commenced. Some general inquiries had been instigated, Thomas Steele who was an undersecretary at the Treasury had made preliminary investigations, and the charges of Thomas Hurd, chief surveyor on Cape Breton until the governor deposed him, had been proved false. DesBarres was back again in the governmental game of pass the petitioner.

The colonial secretary had reported to the Treasury that more than £7,000 was due to the governor for disbursements incurred in Cape Breton before March 25, 1786.[33] Three years later nothing had been paid, although charges, damages, and interest on unliquidated bills at the rate of £870 each year had accumulated.[34] When the Treasury received Sydney's report it was declared too vague, yet DesBarres was allowed to see neither this nor a copy of the charges leading to his recall. Late in 1789, Steele recommended to Pitt, then First Lord of the Treasury and Chancellor of the Exchequer, that something should be done to hold off the petitioner's creditors. In December, £10,000 was placed in the hands of bankers to pay bills DesBarres had drawn in Cape Breton, with 5 percent per annum being allowed for "noting, protests, and interest."[35] When the creditors proved reluctant to give up the property in Nova Scotia which they had seized on DesBarres' failure to pay his debts, altercations ensued and an arbitration board was established with Sir William Dolben and Sir Herbert Mackworth as its leading members. The Treasury's award was used to pay off debts of £7,171 with accumulated interest and fees. As much again remained unpaid.

A good example of the wild paper chases on which supplicants were sent began with the appointment of Henry Dundas as Home Secretary in the Pitt administration during the summer of 1791. In September DesBarres wrote him a memorial asking for "a trial of the accusations against me as Lieutenant Governor of Cape Breton." Dundas politely passed the matter on to the Treasury which in turn pushed it on to the

32. DesBarres *Statement*, p. 53.

33. DesBarres *Statement*, p. 54.

34. DesBarres *Statement*, p. 49.

35. In February of 1789, the report on the account rendered by DesBarres, which was sent from Lord Sydney's office to the Treasury, showed a total of £19,579.18s.0d., DesBarres, *Statement*, p. 55.

Commissioners for Auditing the Public Accounts to whom DesBarres was told to hand over his accounts and vouchers. He remonstrated that they were either in the Treasury's files or had been transferred to the Auditor's office. They were found and inspected by the Commissioners who then sent a list of queries and a request for receipts not found. He replied that he was hardly responsible for the losses of others but in February 1792 Wigglesworth, the Inspector General of the Public Accounts, ruled that without vouchers nothing would be paid, unless there was an order from the Court of Exchequer.

The race was on again. After a declaration from a clerk with the grand title of Keeper of the Treasury Papers, the Exchequer Court gave a ruling during the Hilary term of 1792. The Commissioners did not like it and bombarded DesBarres with more questions "respecting the authority and official formality of the expenditures, accounts, and vouchers." Clearance from the Secretary of State for "home affairs," in charge of colonial administration, saying that there was no complaint from his office against the petitioner, more questions, more delays and, finally, in February 1794, the commissioners signed "a state of your Accounts as Lieutenant Governor of Cape Breton from the 19th November, 1784, to the 13th of October, 1787, with a balance of the sum of £2,213.18s.4¼d., including certain disallowances by way of surcharges."[36] DesBarres was asked for his observations and the auditor even had the gall to tell him to hurry. In August an inquiry took place at the Treasury at which some of the surcharged articles were reviewed and the governor's petitions granted. Others were left unconsidered. After all the procrastinations he was rightly expecting payment but instead he was told that the account could not be settled "until it is lodged in the Pipe Office, where the Quietus must be made out."[37]

Pressed hard by creditors and with hopes of profit from the *Neptune* dashed, he could hardly tolerate all these delays. An acrimonious letter to Dundas and detailed memorials to various departments produced very little. In June 1793 a warrant was issued for the payment of £2,000 to DesBarres as part of the balance due to him, but there is no evidence to show whether or not he was actually paid.[38] A

36. DesBarres *Statement*, p. 72.
37. John Wigglesworth to DesBarres, January 16, 1794, DesBarres, Series V, p. 1930.
38. Transcript of the King's warrant, June 11, 1793, in ibid., p. 1880.

year later William Windham became Secretary at War and Des-Barres' expectations rose, but of course the minister was too busy with weightier matters.[39] Only after Dolben and Mackworth had brought up the question in the House of Commons did Windham ask for copies of the reports of the auditors so that he could "make myself, as much as I can, master of the subject." Rapidly he reached some conclusions. The case could not "possibly be left as it is." DesBarres was "absolutely ruined in consequence of having too well served the Public, and for want of Money, part of which at least is due to him on Grounds, on which it seems impossible to be mistaken." The "formal objections of the Comy of Accounts; whose forms I suspect are very often adverse to substantial Justice" should not be the end of the story.[40]

There was clearly a much better chance of success for DesBarres, who now sought help in a number of places. William Adam, nephew of the celebrated architects and in his own right one of Parliament's most distinguished legal members, offered to provide a professional opinion on the intricate accounts. William Bentinck, relative of the Duke of Portland, captain of the flagship on the Halifax station during 1785 and 1786, and later a governor himself, wrote a long and very favorable testimonial regarding DesBarres' administration. With such support the tone of his petitions became more judicious and he was rewarded with the appointment of William Baldwin, legal counsel to Portland's department of home affairs, to look into the matter. Baldwin's report was one of the most objective commentaries in the huge volume of correspondence which came out of the case. Although the attorney had no personal axe to grind and may have had a leaning toward the government which had given him a profitable position, he found overwhelmingly in favor of the petitioner.

DesBarres' claims may be placed under six headings: (a) expenses resulting from the surveys, of which only £300 was left unpaid, (b) expenses, 1774-1784, totaling £5,475, (c) engraving charts and other connected expenses, of which £3,126.16s.4d. had not been paid, (d)

39. Sir William Dolben advised DesBarres to present a brief case: "All the offices are posses'd of the Detail, and the new Secy wd. not read it if he had it" and, "I cannot but have an opinion that Mr. W. is in earnest himself: how far the old Corps may work upon him remains to be prov'd; if something is not soon done, my doubts or rather despair will return upon me." Dolben to DesBarres, July 21, August 3, 1794, DesBarres Papers, Series V, pp. 1934, 1936.

40. Windham to Charles Long, March 22, 1797, ibid., p. 2096. A copy of the letter was sent to DesBarres.

pay at 20s. a day to 1784, leaving a sum of £1,270 outstanding, (e) the deductions made by the Auditors, amounting to £4,619.1s.5d., and (f) his pay as lieutenant governor, which by this date totaled £5,759.15s.3d.

Baldwin declared that under the first item DesBarres had a right to the interest on the amount and there was "no objection whatever" to the next three items. On the fifth question he censured the commissioners for handling it in far too bureaucratic and legalistic a fashion. Involved in the sixth item was DesBarres' contention that he had not been superseded but only called back to England to explain events in Cape Breton. Counsel did not offer a clear recommendation here but suggested that it had not been made plain to the governor whether or not he had been finally removed from office. The report obtained the approval of both Windham and Portland, but Pitt at the Treasury was not willing to hand over such a large sum and he turned the matter to Thomas Steele, one of his senior assistants. His recommendations were rather less favorable, although he did suggest that DesBarres should receive half the stipend from the time he left the island to 1793.[41]

Steele was not unsympathetic to DesBarres' problems but concluded that he had obtained ample compensation for his surveys, and had been granted all the profit from the publication of the *Atlantic Neptune*, while "the plates were suffered to remain in his hands and to be considered as his property." The claims from the Cape Breton period were a different matter. Steele investigated the circumstances of Des-Barres' appointment and administrative record with considerable thoroughness. He recognized that the "nature of the service . . . was such as not to admit of very precise Instructions from his superior at home and much was therefore left" to the governor's discretion. The difficulties were "so great that every allowance ought to have been made for the irregularities which were found in his accounts." He noted that DesBarres soon after arriving on the island had formed the best possible estimate of his probable expenses and forwarded it to the Secretary of State's office. At first the Treasury had met his charges but later became dissatisfied both with the lack of vouchers and the irregular form of his accounts. In 1786 payment of "several sums on

41. The report is enclosed in Steele to Duke of Portland, June 16, 1801. Brit. Mus. Add. Ms; copy in DesBarres Papers, Series III, pp. 219-29.

account" was refused even though Sydney recommended it and three years later the Treasury was equally adamant when the colonial secretary advised "payment of a great part of" the amount. Steele had to admit that many of the vouchers delivered to both the Treasury and the Secretary of State's office had been lost. DesBarres had said exactly the same thing on many occasions but it must have seemed too partisan to be believable. After the Commissioners for Auditing the Public Accounts authorized a payment of £2,213 DesBarres appealed, the amount was raised to £3,700, and the authorization and DesBarres' remarks on it became the basis for Steele's suggestions.

He found no difficulty in agreeing that it was the duty of the Auditors to watch every penny of public money, but he had also been asked to comment on the equity of the claim. Consequently he felt free to say that in this case a "departure from established rules will not only be justifiable, but laudable, and that considering all the circumstances I have before enumerated, I think he has a fair claim to be allowed the whole sum that is surcharged upon him." A number of exceptions, arising mainly from errors in computations, amounted to only a paltry sum. Charges unsupported by vouchers, to the value of £2,000, were found acceptable, but DesBarres' claim of £1,207 for the period 1763-1773 was totally rejected. In addition to the £2,000 payable without interest, DesBarres could legitimately receive interest at 5 percent on the balance due of the £3,700 already allowed, this to be calculated from the beginning of 1787. Lastly, he was to receive half his salary as lieutenant governor to the end of 1793.[42]

Probably this was the most he could expect but it was far short of his total claims, which had reached as high as £43,000.[43] The always touchy man's reaction was as much on the grounds of character as cash. To Portland he pointed out that his public conduct had been vindicated and he hoped to be restored to his position in Cape Breton, an office from which "I should most probably at this moment have been promoted to that of Nova Scotia, become vacant (as it is said) by the recent recall of Sir John Wentworth."[44] His criticisms were pre-

42. DesBarres received payment at the rate of Halifax currency. The Treasury granted him surcharges of £2,163.7s.8d. Halifax which came to £1,947.0s.11½d. sterling.

43. See memorial of DesBarres to Lords of the Treasury, May 10, 1793, Brit. Mus. Add. Ms, 37890; copy in DesBarres Papers, Series III, p. 215, and Abstract of Advances incurred by Joseph Frederick Wallet DesBarres, Esq., DesBarres Papers, Series V, p. 2145.

44. DesBarres to Duke of Portland, July 4, 1801, ibid., p. 2367. Wentworth did not

sented in courteous and moderate language and were accompanied by an earnest of his continued interests in the Maritimes. He offered a plan for uniting the governments of Cape Breton and Prince Edward, demonstrated their economic relationship with Newfoundland, and proposed that the three islands "should be governed separately from the continental colonies."[45] There was also a suggestion that emphasis should be placed on commerce between British North America and the West Indies in order to drive the Americans out of a profitable carrying trade. At eighty years of age, DesBarres remained incorrigibly enthusiastic and ambitious.

For more than fifteen years he had conducted a remarkable campaign to obtain what he considered his due. He was not an important official. His charts had long since performed their immediate function. Through no fault of his, they had not served a winning side. His one unquestioned accomplishment reminded ministries, which were governing a Britain embroiled in war, of a previous loss to the French. Des Barres could count only Windham as a friend with a voice in the really high places, and although one or two members of Parliament, such as Dolben and Mackworth, helped him, the brunt of the battle was borne by the old man alone. He may have been conceited and cantankerous but he was also courageous and determined. At the age of eighty-three he received the appointment as Lieutenant Governor of Prince Edward Island. Its government was not joined with that of Cape Breton, as he had advised, nor was his former administration vindicated, as he believed, but with the odds heavily against him he had compelled a British government to grant that at least his former errors were not great enough to deny him another colonial position.

---

in fact give up the governorship of Nova Scotia until 1808. For much of his term there was gossip about his wife who had been the mistress of Prince William Henry (later William IV) and rumors of the governor's recall or retirement.

45. "Plan for uniting Cape Breton and Prince Edward Islands," DesBarres Papers, Series V, p. 2462. The plan is undated but was probably written sometime between 1801 and 1803.

CHAPTER VI

A Second Chance

FROM the sky the crescent-shaped island of Prince Edward presents almost a checkerboard pattern of lush green grasslands and red ploughed fields. Here and there a clear blue stream tinkles down to broad sandy beaches washed by the temperating Gulf Stream. The tiny island, little more than two thousand square miles, is Canada's smallest province. Norsemen may well have sailed in the surrounding waters but they left us no record of what they saw. The first important narrative of European discovery comes from Jacques Cartier who passed along its northern coast in his voyage of 1534. Almost two centuries went by before his country paid the island any attention but when the French lost Acadie in the Treaty of Utrecht (1713) they were allowed to retain Île Royale (Cape Breton) and Île St. Jean (Prince Edward). These were precisely the two colonies DesBarres later administered. There was some continuous and permanent settlement after 1719 when a land grant was made to the Comte de Saint Pierre. However, most efforts were concentrated on Louisbourg and by 1752 the population of Île St. Jean was still only two thousand or so.[1] In the next couple of years this figure more than doubled as the British, pressing on with their development of Nova Scotia, pushed out the French-speaking inhabitants. In the second half of the 1750's this process continued but no longer to the advantage of the island. The forced evacuation of the Acadians, so tearfully portrayed in Longfellow's "Evangeline," struck it in 1758 when a small British military party under Lord Rollo was sent from Cape Breton. By the time the colony officially became a British possession in the peace of 1763 less than three hundred Acadians remained.

Whitehall was convinced that the French had prized the island greatly and on this mistaken assessment based high estimates of its future.[2] Many schemes for its development were proposed to the

1. Census of the Sieur de la Roque printed in *Report on Canadian Archives* (Ottawa, 1905), II, 77-165.

2. Edward Boscawen to William Pitt, Earl of Chatham, September 13, 1758, C. O. 412, quoted in Daniel C. Harvey, *The French Regime in Prince Edward Island* (New Haven, 1926), pp. 194-95. Boscawen based his letter on a report from Lord Rollo, who had been

Board of Trade, none being more preposterous than the one of the Earl of Egmont who wanted to reproduce a mediaeval society in the Gulf of St. Lawrence.[3] Rejecting such fantasies, the government utilized the facts in a survey done by Samuel Holland in 1764-1766. The limits of the land grants generally followed his division of the island into sixty-six townships or lots of approximately 20,000 acres, leaving aside three town sites with their additional "royalities" of pasture and garden areas. After lots 40 and 59 had been given to two groups which since 1764 had been involved in trading and fishing activities on the island and Township 66 had been reserved for the Crown, a lottery was used to decide among many petitioners previously approved by the Board of Trade. At one stroke the entire colony was divided and its future placed in the hands of an unconnected body of proprietors. This drastic "solution" of the difficulties inherent in land distribution imposed a problem which handicapped inhabitants and hamstrung governors for more than a century.

The conditions upon which the grants were made are important because their nonfulfillment became the dominant theme in the island's history until Confederation (1867). Laid down by the Board of Trade before the lottery took place, they demanded of the grantees: (a) payment of the quitrents as assessed by the imperial Orders in Council, i.e., from two to six shillings per hundred acres according to locality, fertility, etc., (b) the settling of one person per two hundred acres within ten years, one-third of the land to be settled in this fashion within four years and, (c) that all settlers be Protestants not from His Majesty's dominions, except persons who had resided in the American colonies for two or more years. Thirty years later there was not a soul in twenty-three of the lots, twelve others averaged only three families each, and in 1838 Lord Durham found that:

The great bulk of the island is still possessed by absentees, who hold it as a sort of reversionary interest . . . in the mean time, the inhabitants of the island are subjected to the greatest inconvenience, nay, to the most serious injury from

---

sent by General Jeffrey Amherst to take possession of the island in 1758. Rollo seems to have replaced his ignorance with a much too rapid acceptance of the facts presented to him and an inflated estimate of the island's resources.

3. John Perceval, 2d Earl of Egmont, *To the King's Most Excellent Majesty, the Memorial of John, Earl of Egmont* (London, 1764). Egmont, First Lord of the Admiralty, probably had this printed after the presentation of his third memorial to the King in February 1764. Copy in Rare Book Room, Yale University Library.

the state of property in land. The absent proprietors neither improve the land, nor will let others improve it.[4]

Had the terms of the land grants been met, about 13,000 settlers would have arrived in the first ten years, and the economic history of the island might have been substantially changed. Obtaining such an influx would not perhaps have been impossible, although it certainly would have demanded a concerted effort by the proprietors. But they made no real attempt either to exploit the vast reservoir of prospective emigrants in Europe and the British Isles or to meet the terms of their grants. What they did win for the colony was a period of independence within the imperial system.[5] The Board of Trade, with a carelessness and lack of concern not untypical of its general operations at this time, agreed to this because it offered an easy escape from the dilemma of retaining the island without spending very much extra money. By accepting that administrative expenses could be met through the quitrents during the first ten years, the British government, having recently passed through the troubles of the Stamp Act crisis in the Thirteen Colonies, abdicated responsibility in a new possession instead of using the opportunity to reassess the purposes and the methods of imperial administration. Furthermore, the machinery to support this weak policy was itself haphazard. No practical provision was made for the payment of the quitrents and the proprietors naturally showed no enthusiasm to fulfill their obligations when they were not prodded to do so.

The first British governor, Walter Patterson, was sworn in on August 4, 1769 but did not arrive on the island until a year later. Like those who succeeded him he found himself caught in the middle. On

4. The earlier figures are from John Stewart, *An Account of Prince Edward Island in the Gulph of St. Lawrence, North America* (London, 1806), pp. 220-21. These figures came from an inquiry by the House of Assembly. The quotation is from John George Lambton, 1st Earl of Durham to Charles Grant, Baron Glenelg, October 8, 1838, quoted in Andrew H. Clark, *Three Centuries and the Island* (Toronto, 1959), p. 51. This document was included in the famous report; see Charles P. Lucas (Ed.), *Lord Durham's Report* (3 vols.; Oxford, 1912), II, 242. The proprietors naturally voiced their views less frequently and less vehemently than the island's inhabitants, but Durham's stature brought forth a defense of their position, *Facts versus Lord Durham: Remarks upon that Portion of the Earl of Durham's Report Relating to Prince Edward Island . . . by a Proprietor* (London, 1839).

5. Their petition, made on June 13, 1768, is printed in Frank MacKinnon, *The Government of Prince Edward Island* (Toronto, 1951), pp. 6-7, hereafter cited as MacKinnon, *Government*. See also the commentary in *Acts of the Privy Council, Colonial Series* (London, 1912), V, 82-85.

the one hand, the inhabitants demanded security of tenure, opportunity for agricultural expansion, and a fairer division of the costs of government, on the other, the absent landlords used every possible device of an established patronage system to minimize their expenses, secure "composition" of quitrents long overdue, and maintain their influence in the island's administration. One result of this situation was that Patterson and his subordinates went unpaid for many years, and the governor felt himself forced to appropriate to his own use funds specifically voted for public works projects. This procedure helped to bring about his recall in 1786. His successor, Edmund Fanning, did better in keeping a hold on the slippery ground between the interests of the settlers and the proprietors, although in doing so he had to beat down charges brought against him in a committee of the Privy Council.

DesBarres, the next man on the firing line, was in office for eight years (1804-1812) without any dispute crucial or heated enough to cause him serious trouble. His eagerness to make the most of this second opportunity as an administrator was reflected in the rapidity with which he tackled problems. Rightly believing that the size of the difficulties had to be known before methods could be devised, he initiated a census. Before the end of 1805 he was able to forward to the authorities at home a return of the population, a revision of the return, and an extremely detailed account of acreages under different crops, yields per acre, annual volume of produce, and number of live-stock.[6] Less than six months after his arrival DesBarres and his superiors had a thorough picture of the island's economy. For a man in his eighties it was a remarkably energetic start, but his determined efforts to obtain data, analyze causes, and suggest solutions continued throughout his administration. The opposition this time, unlike his Cape Breton years, was neither strong nor successful. Some in the small group which comprised the island's political leadership were against him before he arrived, simply because he represented imperial authority, and others, who had been intimately aligned with Fanning,

6. A draft history of the quitrent controversy for the years 1790 to 1803 will be found in DesBarres Papers, Series V, pp. 2546-2584. In providing such rapid statistics DesBarres appears to have been aided by the information obtained from a circular of William Sabatier on behalf of the compilers of a proposed history of the island. The governor's report is in DesBarres to Camden, August 6, December 4, 1805. Original Correspondence, Secretary of State—Prince Edward, Colonial Office 226, hereafter C. O. 226.

expected a change of governor to mean a loss of favor. Until the very last part of his tenure DesBarres added no one of consequence to the ranks of opponents while injecting new dynamism and constructive vigor into the hardened arteries of the colony's political life.

DesBarres came at an important point in the island's history. Governor Fanning in a speech to the Assembly in 1802 had told the members that he knew the colony's affairs had been brought to the attention of the King's ministers "in a manner highly favourable to the representations made, respecting the many large unsettled and uncultivated tracts of land in the Island." So hopeful was he of the success of the legislature's demand for a Court of Escheat that he advised it to be ready to adopt the necessary measures for revesting in the Crown those lands which had been forfeited. A bill for such a purpose was passed and received the governor's consent on April 2, 1803 but, despite the hopes raised by Secretary Hobart's promise, it was disallowed in Britain. A committee of the Assembly remonstrated that the assent had been given even if the formal royal allowance had been withheld because of backstairs proprietary influence. A new bill, similar to the old one, was drawn up and passed. Just before DesBarres' appointment, therefore, the islanders had been riding a wave of hope with regard to their perennial problems of land tenure, quitrents, and escheats. Unfortunately their expectations were quickly dashed on the treacherous sands of Court intrigue and an undertow of disappointment was carried over into the new administration. There was one development to offset the bad news on escheats. Thomas Douglas, 5th Earl of Selkirk, provided the single most important influx of immigrants since 1767 when he settled a colony of Highland Scotsmen in 1803.[7] It appeared that after years of obscurity the island was finally winning some attention.

DesBarres quickly appreciated that the colony was backward internally as well as in its connections within the imperial system. Indeed, problems of communication occupied a great deal of his energies through his entire administration. Two specific matters, the improvement of mail service to Nova Scotia in winter and the maintenance of

7. See the diary of Selkirk edited by Patrick C. White (Toronto, 1958) which is the finest nonofficial record of economic conditions in Prince Edward Island for the years immediately preceding DesBarres' arrival. Selkirk's *Observations on the Present State of the Highlands* (London, 1805), pp. 189-219, also offers comments on the settlement of the island.

the island's roads during the summer, loomed as principal troubles. Governor Patterson had been successful in sending his winter dispatches by canoe to the Nova Scotia shore and from there overland to Halifax, but this route was hazardous and expensive and no regular service was established. The colony's first postmaster was not appointed until 1801, almost a decade and a half after the first printer set up shop, but this seems to have increased rather than diminished the cries of dissatisfaction.[8] In 1802, the Assembly complained that letters for the colony were enclosed in the Halifax mail and "left in the post there, exposed, from whence they have been committed to the custody of any individual willing to take charge of them." In the next five years a number of suggestions were made to solve what should not have been a terribly difficult or expensive matter, yet no great improvement resulted. In 1807 DesBarres recommended a packet boat of not less than thirty-five tons to operate between Charlottetown and Tatamagouche, with fares of ten shillings for an adult, five shillings for a child, and fifteen shillings for a horse. But next year he was writing to the chief justice, who was in Halifax at the time, that "nearly five months have elapsed since a line from England has reached this Island; judge then how comfortable any intelligence from there will be to us."[9]

DesBarres' pride as an engineer was even more keenly aroused by the problem of the roads. He was especially concerned with how best to use the statute labor, that is, the citizen manpower made available for limited annual service in public works, under various laws. Given the relatively primitive state of the economy and the lack of both private and public capital, the labor force was the vital factor and its efficient use an issue for the governor's attention. In addition, its organization was closely linked with the training of the militia and involved touchy questions of status, prestige, and local administrative control. Any proposals for change would almost automatically provide new opportunities for the factionalism to which Prince Edward's economic and political leadership was always prone. This had been shown in the history of the various plans to tackle the building of roads, one

8. See Olga B. Bishop, *Publications of the Governments of Nova Scotia, Prince Edward Island and New Brunswick, 1758-1952* (Ottawa, 1957), p. 100.

9. See also "Representation . . . respecting the regular conveyance of letters to and from Halifax" in Prince Edward B, Executive Council Minutes (PAC transcripts), September 15, 1807, hereafter cited as Executive Council Minutes.

means of developing a sense of unity in the colony. Patterson had pointed out to the Colonial Office that the outlying sections could only be reached by water; by land it sometimes took two weeks to travel from Charlottetown to Princetown, even though they were both centers of population and less than fifty miles apart. He wanted to make a road to connect them together, but had to do it on his own initiative and at his own risk.[10] The system of statute labor which he introduced was continued by his successor, Edmund Fanning.

DesBarres made no changes for some time, but early in 1807 he launched a new offensive on the old problem. First he asked for a list of the overseers of the highways for the previous three years.[11] Within two weeks there followed a command that the overseers should let the clerk of the Council know where the labor had been used in the preceding year and indicate the most advantageous areas of work for the current one. No vital departure from the past policies was involved in this, but the pace and the tone of the governor's actions show his constant concern with efficiency and his growing irritation at seeing an important economic matter being made a political football. The House of Assembly supported DesBarres and voted considerable sums for the development of the road system.[12] The Council also was stirred and suggested that the governor "should order advertisements to be put for proposals to make and repair such roads and bridges as His Excellency shall deem most urgent to be made and repaired in the several counties."[13]

No evidence indicates that DesBarres personally benefited from the road-building programs although his son James, as a militia officer, took part in executing them. Nor did the members of the Council derive any extensive personal advantage. But it is equally true that despite all the planning and persuading the efforts to establish a good network of roads on the island was not a brilliant success. In a message to his Council in January 1810 DesBarres felt compelled to put matters bluntly. The "fund of this colony, for last year, if it had been

10. Governor Walter Patterson to Willis Hill, 2d Viscount Hillsborough, July 24, 1771, C. O. 226. In 1771 the Secretary was Viscount Hillsborough in the Irish peerage; in the next year he was created Earl of Hillsborough in the British peerage.

11. Executive Council Minutes, February 3, March 4, 1807.

12. For example, in April 1809, the Lower House voted £150 for the militia and in the same month the Upper House resolved to advise an expenditure of not less than £200. Ibid., October 23, 1809.

13. Ibid., September 5, 1809.

properly called forth, would have amounted to no less than four thousand pounds, one half in money and the other half in statute labour." Five years as governor had convinced him that "this fund has not been advantageously appropriated and that it will continue under the same disadvantage until a new arrangement shall take place." Nothing effective had been done about building a jail or repairing the wharf at Charlottetown and only four miles of new roads had been opened in the previous year. Although one might grant that the island's few artificers had little knowledge or capital, they would be less reluctant to tender for work if they were certain of obtaining materials. A couple of concrete proposals followed. Firstly, "livestock might be brought from the continent, lumber should be contracted for at the sawmills, brickmakers and bricklayers might be found in Nova Scotia and New Brunswick." Secondly, advertising for new men and materials would not be enough. To what must have been a shocked Council DesBarres pointed out that not one overseer had been fired although the conduct of overseers was "perpetually complained of," bridges were erected with no advance planning, and there was generally a dreadful waste of the precious statute labor. He therefore proposed the appointment of an Inspector of Public Works to direct the whole system, with the obligation of reporting to the governor and Council.

Remembering the island's poverty, the willingness to spend large sums and the continuous concern with the state of the roads can be best understood as part of anxiety about defense. The governor saw the two questions as complementary, so much so that he adopted the militia organization for the more efficient use of the statute labor. In 1809, for example, the assignments were divided by regiments, one each for Queen's County North, Queen's County South, King's County, and Prince County.[14] Each regiment was further divided into companies ranging from thirty to sixty-five men, each having its own instructions. Both activities stood to gain by DesBarres' interest and stress on regulation. Ever since the new House Assembly, which had been summoned at the end of 1806, presented the governor with a memorial on the defenseless state of the colony he had been simultaneously trying to rouse Whitehall and raise the island's own

14. Ibid., August 29, 1809.

power.[15] The statute labor-road building policy of 1809 was an attempt to introduce military precision into a critical civil concern.

Although most of DesBarres' suggestions were sound, they created some differences. As early as 1806 he found himself in the middle of a jurisdictional dispute caused, as was the one in Cape Breton twenty years before, by a combination of imperial maladministration and local political rivalries. Charles Stewart, a leader of the most powerful family in the island, refused to permit the colony's Commissioners for Auditing the Public Accounts to see his papers as Deputy Receiver General of the Quitrents. Declaring that his appointment was made by the Treasury, he claimed that he did not need to show his records to any Colonial Office appointee. Even after parts of the governor's Instructions were read to him—a procedure the home authorities would not have liked—he remained adamant. In the Cape Breton days DesBarres would have pushed the problem to a stage of acidic division; now he allowed it to fizzle out.

Stewart was also chairman of an extragovernmental committee of correspondence, which functioned as an out of session extension of the House of Assembly. It came to the governor's attention officially through a letter sent to him by William Knox, the colony's agent in London.[16] When the Council requested to see the correspondence with Knox, Stewart refused to comply on the grounds that consent of the House was necessary. Under DesBarres' guidance the Council wisely decided that if Knox were told the full circumstances he would close his end of the correspondence. In striking contrast to his attitude on Cape Breton, the governor was cooly avoiding legalistic but impractical disputes. Similarly, he made no extravagant claims and modified those of others. In October 1806, the DesBarres-led Council resolved that Knox had been deceived as to the actual state of the colony and declared that, in reality, there were only forty miles of road open for carriages in the summer, only two public buildings, a church erected by private subscription, and a jail incapable of housing prisoners.[17] Simultaneously, a promise was made that a bill would be prepared and laid before the next session of the General Assembly which would be "calculated to remove the obstacles which have heretofore retarded

15. Address of the House of Assembly, December 16, 1806, C. O. 226.
16. Executive Council Minutes, September 12, 1806.
17. Ibid., October 18, 1806.

the progress of this island." It would obviously be still another attempt to alter the quitrent situation.

The longest and most serious argument in which DesBarres was involved began with his 1810 proposals for better use of the statute labor. Chief Justice Caesar Colclough came to the somewhat curious conclusion that the programs were affronts to himself. He then refused to accept responsibility for the expenditures already made and completely rejected the governor's new plans, stressing his belief that the administration could not hire fine craftsmen or bring limestone from either Nova Scotia or New Brunswick. In essence Colclough was in favor of the status quo ante DesBarres, because he saw the possibility of political agitation resulting from the governor's ideas. His advice that more attention might be paid to the feelings of the House which even if it "has not the auditing of the revenue, yet it has the auditing of the accounts and the power of commenting on the expenditure" was sensible but not very necessary. The Assembly had shown no greater opposition to DesBarres' earlier proposals than it had to those of Fanning whose administration had been long enough and quiet enough to induce the British government to grant him a full pension. As for Colclough's advice that the Council's support was important "since the governor cannot issue a warrant to the treasurer for even a single dollar without the advice and consent of the council," this had been given even on measures which the chief justice now said he opposed.[18]

It is by no means certain what policy Colclough favored, other than that of not kicking up trouble at home. His correspondence contained a confused mixture of passive pessimism and stolid obstruction. He admitted that there was no constitutional objection to the idea of central direction but left unclear whether he was offended by the matter or the method. Perhaps he himself did not know but, whatever the case, his remarks were the first thin rattle in the battle he launched against the governor. Alexander Howe, a friend of the chief justice, suggested that DesBarres was showing unnecessary liberality in throwing away public monies. Since Howe was a member of the Council which, as Colcough had taken pains to point out, had to give its consent before the governor could dispose of funds, his insinuation was weak and self-serving.

18. Ibid., 1806-1810, passim.

A Second Chance

The most wholehearted supporter of DesBarres was James Palmer who did not join the Council until October 1809. He strongly urged that improvements must be made and unequivocably declared that the scheme would be accepted by the House and found efficient by the island. Action was needed and the governor had shown the way by reducing the cost of the previous year's work by thirty percent and raising the fine paid by those wishing to be excused from statute labor.[19] Palmer encouraged DesBarres with the observation that just as "the militia establishment was new, so was the regular conveyance of letters, so is the present proposed appointment, the house of assembly inquired and approved, and they will again." In May 1810 there arrived a letter from the Earl of Liverpool stating that royal approval had been given to the Assembly's act "for raising the sum of £1,600 for the purpose of erecting buildings for the meeting of the general assembly, the supreme court and its officer . . . and for building two gaols."

This was the signal for a spate of planning. Estimates for building a courthouse were received, orders given for opening a further six miles of the West road, and detailed proposals submitted for using the statute labor. As evidence that these new preparations should overcome old antagonisms DesBarres appointed both Colclough and Palmer to the commission for erecting Charlottetown's public buildings. In the emphasis on efficiency no one was beyond the governor's control. Palmer's request in October 1810 for fifty pounds as one year's pay was declared unacceptable "until that officer renders a specific account of services performed as adjutant general of militia." Another supporter, Thomas Desbrisay, found his memorial for official fees referred until it was found out whether the royal assent had ever been given to the Fee Act of 1776.

During his last two years as governor DesBarres lost some of the impartial stance he had hitherto been able to maintain. Inevitably, this happened when he became involved in the problem of the quit-rents, the most protracted and pestilential political question on the island. For more than half a decade the governor had cleverly avoided the camps of both settlers and proprietors but between 1810 and 1812 there took place an unprecedented attack on the stultifying policies of

19. The fine was raised from 5s. to 16s.; the daily wage of laborers, improved by competition from the timber trade, was 8s. per day, according to Palmer.

[89]

the absentee landlords. Before it was over, the chief justice was transferred to Newfoundland and the Loyal Electors, headed by Palmer, took fleeting hold on the Assembly. Some years before his appointment DesBarres, from an interested and informed position as a Maritimes landowner constantly involved in lawsuits, had favored the proprietary cause and even written a long treatise on landlord-tenant relationships.[20] He was opposed to the hopes raised by Fanning, likening them to "the chaotic dreams of all levellers in all ages." He thought there was some small virtue in the court of escheat established in Nova Scotia, but every such instrument infused "too much cupidity for what belongs to others" and tended to become the means whereby idle fellows attacked their landlords for not complying with impossible conditions dictated by impractical governments.[21] In Prince Edward the court would do little more than sanction thievery since it would be administered by those standing to gain directly by any forfeitures. Such views, when added to his intense dislike of "factions," seemed to preclude open opposition to the proprietorial interests, yet the last part of DesBarres' administration is notable because it saw the real beginning of political parties on Prince Edward, centered around the issues of land tenure and local control.

Prior to his arrival he had formed an unflattering estimate of the "illiterate" Assembly and masterfully ridiculed its claim, in the *Resolves* of 1797, that the island could house a population of half a million. On the other hand, he regarded a man such as John Stewart, Speaker of the House and Receiver General of Quitrents, as spearheading a pro-proprietorial oligarchy which usually knew how to "pack the cards and play into one another's hands as they might please." After becoming governor he listened to many advisers. One of these was Palmer, whom on one occasion he used as an agent for his lands in Nova Scotia, but there is no evidence that he was dominated by the younger man and seduced into accepting the Loyal Electors.

20. The incomplete draft history of the controversy covering the years 1790 to 1803 occupies most of Volume 8 in Series V of the DesBarres Papers. Much of the discussion of DesBarres' views is based upon this.

21. DesBarres, in a remarkably fair appraisal, disputed the claim that the prosperity of Nova Scotia and New Brunswick was due to the operation of the Court of Escheat. Up to 1782 the rural inhabitants in Nova Scotia were no more prosperous than those in Prince Edward Island, but the state of the economy was significantly altered by the influx of Loyalists whose accommodation was beneficially influenced by the existence of such a court. See DesBarres Papers, Series V, pp. 2546-84.

DesBarres had suffered all his life for his strong opinions and tendency to see matters in black and white, and while old age may have mellowed him a trifle the frequent testimonies to his continued vigor strongly refute any picture of a doddering governor at the mercy of scheming politicians.

The standard explanation that a man speaks through one side of his mouth out of office and through the other when in power is hardly a better answer. DesBarres, in effect, had persistently criticized both factions on the island and then after his appointment as governor labored to make them work together. In the position he took after coming to Prince Edward one may detect a broader interest than his sympathy with the proprietors. His overriding concern was the prosperity of Prince Edward. As a result DesBarres, who had previously shown absolutely no talent at staying within the bounds of imperial instructions, could suggest that his predecessor Fanning should have asked the home government to examine the general state of the colony instead of haranguing the multitude, as he believed the governor had done. DesBarres had even developed some sense of imperial priorities. He expressed opposition to schemes for bringing out Scottish emigrants because this would be a drain on Britain's vitally needed manpower and proposed that, for the moment at least, "the settlement go softly on, as it might, by the local increase."

So far as possible he tried to let sleeping issues lie, apparently bearing in mind the chief lesson of his Cape Breton administration. Whitehall required an unimportant colony to remain untroublesome. DesBarres could see, far more clearly than he had done a quarter of a century earlier, that "the object of the Old Country . . . is not so much the benefit of the individuals who may be placed there, as the advantage it may produce to the parent state." In an island where estates of 20,000 acres were being offered for £50, where in three years "not a sixpence of revenue has been received, or at least, it has not been accounted for," with an economy which scarcely produced a surplus, it was useless to expect that a quitrent of even £100 could be paid. If the quitrents had not been collected during the American Revolution when British forces temporarily boosted the Maritimes economy and made local prices soar, what chance was there now of collecting either current amounts or the massive arrears.

In the first six years of his administration DesBarres, resisting the more drastic schemes of Palmer, concentrated on internal reforms and more efficient use of the island's resources. He had not perhaps greatly changed as a person—Colclough for one complained of his arbitrary manners—but he now had himself far more in check even though he had met with only limited success and found himself, as his predecessors had done, up against a solid wall of resistance. However, the death of Peter MacGowan, the attorney general in June 1810, provided a focus for the seemingly endemic personal rivalries on the island. DesBarres wrote that "a colonial education, and particularly in this infant place, can afford but little knowledge in theory and still less in practice. One hundred pounds would purchase in England a better selection of law books than the joint stock of all the judges and lawyers in this island would exhibit."[22] He expressed a desire for someone of "British education and practical experience," and then briefly described the training, career, and qualities of half a dozen of the island's lawyers. Palmer was commended "as a laborious individual, unembarrassed with extraneous concerns," which was comparatively true since his most serious rival, Charles Stewart, was Collector of the Revenue, Deputy Receiver General of the Quitrents and agent for several proprietors. Robert Hodgson, another possible choice, was Speaker of the House. On the other hand, Lord Selkirk was in favor of Stewart as being the most acceptable to the proprietors and regarded Palmer as "extremely objectionable in every respect."[23]

The Society of Loyal Electors, which had existed on the island from at least the early summer of 1809, saw Stewart as its principal antagonist. The organization was the product of Palmer's impatient mind, and in the words of one of its members was designed to bring about "the introduction of upright independent men and persons of unimpeached character into the House of Assembly with a view of counteracting a dangerous influence . . . possessed by a set of persons engaged in monstrous speculations in land."[24] Certainly even by 1805, when he had been on the island three years, Palmer had come to feel that changes in the membership of the House would be an improvement.

22. DesBarres to Liverpool, July 3, 1810, C. O. 226.

23. Selkirk to Liverpool, March 2, 1811, C. O. 226.

24. Statement on oath of William Roubel, September 17, 1811, C. O. 226. Roubel was a lawyer who had served his apprenticeship in London, been admitted as a barrister on the island in 1808, and served in the Assembly before returning to England late in 1811.

Colclough and other timid souls were alarmed. Britain was in mortal combat with a nation which had spread the cry of revolution throughout Europe. In North America, memories of an earlier "leveling" revolution were even keener. Members of the society were at particular pains to protest that it was neither a secret organization nor a "Political Correspondence Club," and stressed it was "a *Loyal* association assembling on truly British, constitutional principles."

Colclough disagreed, and the issue exacerbated the antagonism between him and the governor. More importantly, the island's troubles reached Whitehall's eyes, mainly through the letters of the chief justice who also contacted a few of the proprietors.[25] A general election was held in April 1812, but Palmer and his successful Loyal Electors received little chance to carry through any reforms because in August DesBarres was recalled and Charles Smith was appointed as his successor. In the interim, the island's government was to be exercised by the second member of the Council, "it being deemed incompatible that the Senior Member should be placed in that situation whilst he fills the office of secretary and register." On the same day as DesBarres was recalled, a letter was sent from Downing Street to Townshend, the temporary executive, ordering him to relieve Palmer of his office. The complaints of the chief justice would not have been enough to bring about such drastic remedies in a minor colony, but a combination of proprietary pressure and the war with the United States were more significant factors to be considered.

DesBarres had been influenced by Palmer but not dominated by him. Any movement which could seriously hurt the proprietors aroused fear in an agent such as Charles Stewart or a conservative such as Colclough, who tried to improve his position by becoming their principal informant. One proprietor, a London merchant by the name of Hill, demanded the governor's removal, claiming that he was in "absolute dotage" and completely in the hands of Palmer, "an absolute swindler." He must have been well aware that accusing Palmer and the settlers of a "tendency to Jacobinical principles" would be damning, particularly when he could link this with the formation of a fifth column to welcome "an invasion of the Republican

25. Colclough to Robert Banks Jenkinson, 2d Earl of Liverpool, August 23, 1810, C. O. 226.

Americans."[26] Yet DesBarres' second chance in the administration was far from a dismal failure; by comparison with his spleenish tenure in Cape Breton it was a notable success. The population and some public buildings had gone up. Even the erection of a hotel was contemplated. The island's systems of communications and defense had been reorganized, not fully by any means, but creditably in the circumstances. For much of the time there had been comparative political peace before the governor finally fell afoul the old issue of quitrents, as previous governors had done. This, together with the imminence of a war with the United States, meant that a younger and more martial figure was needed. The nonagenarian governor had reason to be proud. He had done more than his superiors saw, possibly even more than he himself recognized, in throwing the weight of gubernatorial support to the formation of the first real political party in the island, the first valiant and self-conscious step toward "responsible government" in Prince Edward Island's troubled history.

26. In the absence of any other detailed account of DesBarres' administration, it is unfortunate that Hill's *ex parte* statements have been repeated, without note of the prejudiced character of the source, in MacKinnon, *Government*, p. 54. One of Hill's claims was that the Society was "composed chiefly of Americans." He gave no proof of this and the available records provide no support for his accusation.

Epilogue

AFTER his retirement from colonial administration, at the age of ninety, DesBarres left Charlottetown and crossed the Northumberland Strait to his farm near Amherst, Nova Scotia, where he lived until 1817 when he moved to Halifax. A son, James Luttrell, was sent to London with the governor's last dispatches and orders to improve the family's financial position. After his arrival in June 1813 his efforts were directed toward increasing his father's pension, obtaining documents which would protect the estates from further attacks in the New Brunswick courts, and finding a buyer for the plates of the *Atlantic Neptune*.[1] Naturally, this last activity resurrected the question of ownership.[2] When DesBarres heard about the publication of charts either copied from the *Neptune* or heavily indebted to it he was very upset and protested that it was an infringement of his rights.[3] But the matter was not quite that simple. In an era when even a writer lacked the protection of a clear, well-enforced copyright law the hydrographer was in a very ambiguous situation. DesBarres was finding that the uncertainty which had been beneficial when the charts were initially published was now working against him.

James received the help of John Elliott, a London brewer with whom DesBarres had left many of his charts and the original plates before he went to Prince Edward Island, in his attempts to obtain estimates of the value of the *Neptune* from London's principal chart makers. The two men also entertained the idea of selling the plates to the Admiralty which thereby found itself in a strange position. While it continued to claim the charts as its own, it ordered the official hydrographer to report on their utility and worth as a first step in considering purchase. Meanwhile James asked DesBarres for permission to publish the charts at his own expense. He also offered to buy the *Neptune* on credit, paying back the price at the rate of eight hundred pounds a year. Neither scheme was very practical

1. He was to be paid £500 plus expenses, DesBarres Papers, Series I, p. 663.

2. James told his father in an undated letter, received January 1814 that the Admiralty considered the copyright its own and it had "the right to repudiate the work when they choose," DesBarres Papers, Series V, p. 4647.

3. James reported that a Mr. Steel had recently published charts for the coast from the Straits of Belle Isle to the Gulf of Mexico, declaring them to be "taken from the surveys of Desbarres & others," James L. DesBarres to DesBarres, July 9, 1813, ibid., p. 4749. Steel was probably one of the partners in the chart-selling firm R. and D. Steel (London). See Adrian H. W. Robinson, *Marine Cartography in Britain* (Leicester, England, 1962), p. 123.

and the son, who had inherited an eye for a quick guinea, withdrew his offer when he learned of the possibility of making a fast fortune from trading ventures.[4] In 1814, through the aid of Lord Sidmouth, he was able to wring a promise of an additional two hundred pounds for his father's pension of three hundred pounds per annum, but five years later he reported that over a thousand pounds was outstanding in addition to five hundred pounds from the Prince Edward contingency account.[5]

As for the *Neptune,* matters dragged on from 1813 to 1821, with first James and then his brother Augustus trying to put their father's case before the British government. The negotiations were complicated by a number of factors. In addition to the fundamental question of whether it was Des-Barres or the Admiralty who owned the plates, plans, and charts there were several problems of clashing personalities. The Admiralty placed great store on the advice of Thomas Hurd, the chief of its hydrography department, who happened to have been fired by DesBarres from his position as surveyor general of Cape Breton.[6] On the other side of the bargaining counter James followed his father's example in accepting a high, perhaps even exorbitant, estimate of £40,000 as the value of the work. He also tried to turn a personal profit on it and then finally, without even consulting DesBarres, sold some of the charts to a dealer in Philadelphia.[7] This last action was one of the reasons why his father lost confidence in him, appointed Augustus as one of the executors of his will, and thereafter named the younger boy to sell the *Neptune*.[8] If Augustus was less extravagant in his expectations he was also a poorer businessman. Not as resolute in the face of Admiralty claims, he quickly liquidated this vital asset by selling the copperplates as scrap. We have no exact record of the trans-

4. James's dreams of quick money were shattered in less than two years. The sale of Tatamagouche timber, which was his most tangible project, failed to realize the profits he had hoped. His other ventures were little more than airy ideas. The relevant correspondence is in DesBarres Papers, Series V, pp. 4749-71.

5. James L. DesBarres to DesBarres, January 28, 1814, ibid., p. 4767. The pension was subject to income tax, ibid., p. 4771. On the Prince Edward Island salary see James L. DesBarres to DesBarres, May 14, 1819, DesBarres Papers, Series V, p. 4801. See also a statement of the account April 30, 1819, ibid., p. 4803.

6. James wrote to his father that Hurd was "one of your worst enemies," James L. DesBarres to DesBarres, January 28, 1814, ibid., p. 4767. A friend of James reported that Hurd had "a bastard work of his in Embryo for which he has already received £12,000 with the prospect of drawing an annuity" and therefore sale of DesBarres' *Atlantic Neptune* to the government would be postponed indefinitely. See Henry Chesner to DesBarres, March 7, 1814, ibid., p. 4681.

7. Date of the sale is uncertain, but it probably occurred in 1814, DesBarres Papers, Series I, pp. 245, 605.

8. The will was originally drawn up in March 1818 and restated, without major changes, in October 1824, shortly before DesBarres died. See ibid., pp. 591-609.

action but it seems clear that they went for only £850.7s.6d.[9] This was slightly more than one-fiftieth of James's admittedly ambitious calculation.

DesBarres was still amazingly active. There is even a story, which may not be entirely apocryphal, that he celebrated his hundredth birthday in 1821 by dancing a jig on top of a table. There is no doubt that he remained a lively and cantankerous personality almost to his death at Halifax in 1824, just a month short of his one hundred and third birthday. He established a place for himself in the capital's society, founded the Rockingham Club, and was selected to plan the grounds of Prince's Lodge which was used by the Duke of Kent. He was a leader in the erection of St. George's Church, where he was later buried, and in his typical headstrong fashion made his views prevail over those of anyone else in the congregation. The vigorous individuality of the man seemed unquenchable.

Many of the same characteristics were revealed in his handling of the problems still attending his lands. At the age of ninety-four he toured the estates and from then until the end of his life he and his lawyers tried hard, through a series of arbitrations of tenant claims and proposed sales, to turn them from a capital liability into an immediate cash advantage. But since all DesBarres' expenses during the previous half century were in one form or another introduced as the first matter for reimbursement, it became impossible for lessees, who disputed his contention that he had consistently subsidized them and improved the farms, to meet the prices he demanded. He could rant, in his wilder moments, that the tenants were nothing less than "prowling bands of degenerate conspirators, scandalously supported in their iniquitous perpetrations by crafty leaders, interpreters, collectors, treasurers, secretaries, clerks, and other co-operating confederates, sharing in the spoliation of my usurped and mouldering property," but even more sane discussions of terms failed to produce solutions. The net result of the huge investments in Maritimes real estate was a legacy of lawsuits which embroiled his family for a good deal of the nineteenth century.

The children also inherited DesBarres' quarrelsome disposition. The substitution of Augustus for James in the father's favor created a major feud, while five sisters were constantly haranguing both each other and their brothers. DesBarres who, as the years went by, became increasingly concerned with providing for his children, especially the girls, reminded the family that he had "experienced much trouble and perplexity in the management of my real estates in British North America" and suggested that they should band together and sell the estates as quickly as possible. He decreed that his wealth be divided into ten shares, two to be

9. Ibid., p. 250.

given to his wife Martha (about whom we know little more than this isolated fact and that she was eventually buried beside her husband in St. George's, Halifax) and one each to his sons James Luttrell, Augustus Wallet, Dolben Wyndham, and his daughters Martha Frederica [Indiana], Isabella Matilda, Clara, Louisa, and Grace Frederica. Another son, Joseph Frederick, died in India in 1817. In a way he was lucky, for within weeks of their father's death his brothers and sisters were squabbling about their shares and hiring lawyers without a second thought about costs, appearances, or the possibility of settlement. Their quarrel dragged on for forty years with little being gained by anybody.

They were true children of Joseph Frederick Wallet DesBarres. Although not one of them demonstrated a trace of his artistic and technical genius, they all resembled him in a certain pettiness and an eagerness to dispute. In his achievements, however, he towered over them. His careers, spanning nearly seven decades and two continents, were varied enough to be a microcosm of eighteenth century military and administrative life. He topped no peaks of success either as an officer or as a governor, although his career in this latter role provides an intriguing picture of Britain's smaller colonies after the American Revolution, but as the creator of the *Atlantic Neptune* he was responsible for a magnificent work which can clearly be reckoned a classic of hydrographic history. Perhaps we know too little to render any conclusive judgment on his character, but as a public official he was a semitragic figure. A man of great expectations he forever saw his hopes dashed; a man of enormous energies he was rarely rewarded with unqualified approval; an administrator with a keen eye for broad plans and future possibilities, he vitiated his efforts with a personality which called forth envy and dislike rather than admiration and support. Not quite a five-talents man, in the last resort DesBarres' temperament and his financial troubles prevented him from either giving his gifts free rein or achieving a full measure of happiness.

BIBLIOGRAPHICAL ESSAY

Bibliographical Essay

INTRODUCTION

PRIMARILY this study has been based upon two types of manuscript material, the papers of DesBarres and his family and the official records of Cape Breton, Prince Edward Island and, to a lesser extent, Nova Scotia and New Brunswick. The use has been made easier by their availability on microfilm and the unfailing efficiency and courtesy of the Public Archives of Canada (PAC) which, through their own handsome collections and their policy of copying extensively from those elsewhere, greatly facilitate the labors of those interested in Canadian history. Other depositories in Canada, the United States, and Great Britain provided supplementary materials amplifying, corroborating or contradicting the evidence in the private papers and the Colonial Office records.

The DesBarres Papers include photostats of relevant British government records and supplementary material in the same form was obtained from Great Britain by the author. Cape Breton material has been gathered together at the Public Archives of Nova Scotia. Archives for Prince Edward Island have recently been established. The author visited Charlottetown but found no significant new material. Under the aegis of the PAC an union list of manuscripts in Canadian depositories has been prepared. It should be supplemented by scrutiny of reports and other publications issued by the various provincial archives and historical societies. As throughout this work the abbreviations PAC and PANS in the following notes stand for the Public Archives of Canada, Ottawa and the Public Archives of Nova Scotia, Halifax. In addition, MG will stand for manuscript groups at the Canadian archives.

MANUSCRIPTS

1. *DesBarres Papers*

THE total extent of the DesBarres Papers is over seven thousand pages. They may be divided into five series. All material in the first four series, in the sixth series and in twenty-four of the twenty-eight of the volumes in the fifth series is relevant to J. F. W. DesBarres. The DesBarres Papers are listed as item F. 1. in MG 23 at the Public Archives of Canada. Series 1, 3, and 4 are calendared in the *Report of the Public Archives for 1923*, Appendix D, pp. 7-16.

Series I: DesBarres-Ashfield papers. (8 inches.)

Correspondence, 1785-1828; accounts, 1784-1825; miscellaneous papers, 1785-1829; memoranda, 1785-1822; papers relating to DesBarres estates, 1812-1825. This series provides an outline of DesBarres' career. It was heavily relied upon in the only account of DesBarres' life previous to this one, that of John C. Webster.

Series II: John Macdonald's report, 1795. (76 pages.)

Macdonald, a prominent landholder in Prince Edward, made a detailed report (contained in two notebooks) on DesBarres' estates at Minudie, Maccan and Nappan, and Tatamagouche, as they were in 1795. It contains descriptive details not available in the accounts and other financial records in Series V. The MS was acquired by the PAC in 1916.

Series III: Photocopied material, 1774-1807. (4 inches.)

Copies of letters and papers in the British Museum and the Public Record Office, London which relate to DesBarres' hydrographic work.

Series IV: Biographical and genealogical information on DesBarres. (29 pages.)

This is a brief series of papers owned by Rev. Thomas DesBarres. Transcripts for PAC made in 1923.

Series V: This series, containing a collection of papers and correspondence acquired by the PAC in 1958, greatly exceeds the combined volume of the previous four series. It can be most clearly described by stating the contents of the volumes used in this study.

Volumes 1 and 2: Extensive material dealing with the naval surveys and the publication of the *Atlantic Neptune*. Includes correspondence with the naval commander in chief in North America, 1764-1773, and with various departments of the British government, 1773-1814. Of considerable value for chapter V of this study.

Volume 3: Charles Morris and Correspondence received, 1771-1784. Material important for an understanding of DesBarres' real estate investment. Includes letters from Richard Gibbons and others in the Nova Scotia government. Contains valuable comments on the problems of the Surveyor General of Nova Scotia in the period prior to the coming of the Loyalists.

Volumes 4 and 5: An important group of papers dealing with DesBarres' tenure as Lieutenant Governor of Cape Breton. Approximately 400 pages in length, including many items not duplicated in the official records.

Volume 6: Accounts, 1767-1794. This volume, covering pages 1061 to 1380, clearly shows the connection between DesBarres' private estates and his administration in Cape Breton. There are also accounts with various merchants, including Samuel Sparrow, which reveal the connection between DesBarres' mortgages of the *Neptune* and his public accounts.

Volumes 7-12: Representation of his Case. An extensive addition of some 800 pages to the information contained in Series III and volumes 1 and 2 of Series V regarding DesBarres' long fight with the British government to obtain repayment of money spent in public service, mainly during his Cape Breton administration.

Volume 13: Approximately twenty pages of papers relating to a project of Ira Allen and others for a canal linking Lake Champlain and the St. Lawrence River. The second, and much more lengthy, part of the volume deals with the problem of the quitrents on Prince Edward Island. It includes, pp. 2546-84, a draft history of the controversy, written by DesBarres. The papers reflect DesBarres' interest in farming and reveal many imaginative ideas for the more successful development of the island. Most of the papers are from the period before 1804.

Volume 14: Lieutenant Governor of Prince Edward Island, 1804-1812. Approximately 250 pages, of limited value because a large part consists of duplicates of official correspondence. The papers do show the close connection between the ideas of Palmer and DesBarres, a fact not revealed in the Colonial Office records which have hitherto been used exclusively. The volume also contains some information on such local matters as public auctions in Charlottetown.

Volume 15: Land Acquisitions, 1764-1776 and Plans, 1765-1816. This small volume is less important than its title suggests. It contains copies of the orders in Council by which DesBarres received much of his land, and includes papers relating to the purchases he made from fellow grantees. The ten pages of plans are too fragmentary and too limited in scope to be of great value.

Volume 16: Acadia Company, 1775-1785. These papers present solid evidence that DesBarres had personal designs connected with his public service in Cape Breton. They also show his contacts in the lower echelons of several departments in the British government.

Volume 17: Expenses and Agreements with Tenants, 1766-1786. Slightly more than 100 pages in length, with one or two items in French. Unfortunately, the papers from the period before 1773 are little more than accounts and hardly show how DesBarres ran his estates when he himself was in a position to do so.

Volume 18: Mary Cannon and E. Barron, Agents, 1774-1795. Consists of accounts, memoranda, agreements, and leases entered into by DesBarres' agents. Cannon is the person principally involved, and there is little correspondence between Barron and DesBarres or between Barron and anyone else. Approximately 400 pages in length.

Volume 19: Correspondence re Estates, 1795-1812. During this period several persons, including members of his own family, acted as DesBarres' agents. In addition, several lawyers were engaged in various suits for ejectment, trespass, etc., designed to protect DesBarres' estates from forfeiture and to render them as profitable as possible. The volume provides material for an assessment of Cannon's stewardship and a consideration of the multiple factors responsible for the unprofitable condition of the estates. The correspondence has been listed alphabetically by the PAC.

Volume 20: Correspondence, 1795-1812. This is a continuation of volume 19. Together, the two volumes comprise slightly more than a thousand pages. The quantity of material is deceptive. The estate records are fragmentary and the papers concerning lawsuits are often contradictory. In short, both in economic and legal matters it is very difficult indeed to obtain a continuous, consistent, and complete picture of the DesBarres estates.

Volume 21: Tatamagouche Suits, 1809-1813. This brief volume, confined to one of the estates and covering a short period, conveys something of the troubles in which DesBarres found himself as a result of his need to depend on such agents as Cannon and Wellwood Waugh. There is a valuable and comprehensive legal opinion by Richard J. Uniacke.

Volumes 22 and 23: Land Correspondence, 1813-1824. Volume 22 also includes important letters between DesBarres and his son, James Luttrell DesBarres, regarding attempts to sell the plates of the *Neptune*. A large part of the correspondence in these volumes concerns lawsuits. Approximately 1,500 pages in length.

Bibliographical Essay

Volume 28: Genealogical and biographical information on the Des-Barres family. This volume is almost entirely in French. It has little to do with DesBarres directly. Hardly any of the genealogical information deals with the eighteenth century, and it is therefore of limited value for this study.

In addition to furnishing the material for a biography of DesBarres, the Papers provide insights into eighteenth-century hydrographical surveying, into the administration of Cape Breton Island and the settlement of the Loyalists there, into the accumulation and development of estates in the Maritimes, and into the history of Prince Edward Island. Some papers remain in private hands. As far as the DesBarres family in Canada is concerned, it would seem that the principal cache is in the possession of a descendant living in Ontario. I have been denied access to these papers, and their owner is unwilling to indicate either their extent or their general content. Extensive conversation both with him and others convinces me that it is unlikely that when these papers are made available to the historian, if ever they are, they will cause any substantial change in the story as I have told it. What might happen, at some future date, is that a small number of additional details will be presented in a genealogical statement which presently promises to be somewhat hagiographical in nature.

2. Government Papers

Considerable use was made of the wealth of material to be found in the official records and correspondence of the colonies of Cape Breton and Prince Edward. In both cases, the material for ten years preceding Des-Barres' administrations, as well as during them, was read in order to obtain a deeper understanding of the problems which he faced. In the case of Cape Breton this meant, of course, examination of Nova Scotia documents for the period of the governorships of Legge, Arbuthnot, Hughes, Hammond, and Parr (to 1784).

Colonial Office 217 contains the dispatches and enclosures from the governors, lieutenant governors, and other officials of Cape Breton and Nova Scotia. The complete set of 242 volumes, covering the period 1603 to 1867, has been microfilmed. Transcripts of the Nova Scotia correspondence to 1840, and the Cape Breton correspondence from 1784 to 1820 are designated Nova Scotia A and Cape Breton B respectively. The series is composite in nature and is derived from a number of sources in Great Britain. After the PAC had begun its copying work, the Public Record Office created C. O. 217 and the Cape Breton papers are included as a unit at the end of 1819. Accordingly, the papers for the island's administration occur as volumes 103 to 138 in C. O. 217. A calendar of Cape Breton A for the period up to 1801 was published in the 1895 *Report* of the Public Archives. The volumes of the Nova Scotia documents relevant to this study are calendared in the 1894 *Report*.

The complementary papers for Prince Edward Island are gathered together as Colonial Office 226. The entire series for the period 1769 to 1873 has been microfilmed, and there are also forty volumes of transcribed correspondence for the years, 1763-1840, which were called Prince Edward A. The early volumes were composed of documents from both the Public Record Office and the Dartmouth Papers. The papers from the Public Record Office were later grouped together as C. O. 226, and from volume A36 (1820), the A numbering parallels the numbering of C. O. 226. A calendar of Prince Edward A was published in the 1895 *Report*. For volumes 17-40, which include DesBarres' administration, a manuscript calendar is available at the PAC.

For Nova Scotia, Cape Breton, and Prince Edward the second most important records of official actions are the Minutes of the Executive Councils. These are designated Nova Scotia B, Cape Breton B, and Prince Edward B respectively. Each is a composite series which includes material to be found in C. O. 217 and C. O. 226. Nevertheless, it was found that on many important occasions far more detailed information was contained in the Minutes themselves than in the Official Correspondence in which they were transmitted. A calendar of the Nova Scotia series was published in the 1949 *Report* of the PAC. Manuscript calendars for the Cape Breton series are available in Ottawa. Legislative Council Journals and Assembly Council Journals are available for Nova Scotia and Prince Edward during the period of DesBarres' administrations. Cape Breton, lacking a legislative body, does not have such records. The Council Journals are labeled Nova Scotia C and Prince Edward C, the Assembly Journals Nova Scotia D and Prince Edward D. Once again, despite the fact that they are a composite series of transcripts from papers now included in C. O. 217 and C. O. 226, they contain information not present in the correspondence series.

Colonial Office 218 and Colonial Office 227 are the Nova Scotia-Cape Breton and Prince Edward Island Entry Books respectively. These brief series contain copies of outgoing interdepartmental letters and, of more importance for the present study, copies of commissions and instructions from the Board of Trade and the Secretary of State. C. O. 220, Privy Council, Cape Breton, 1785-1795, is both brief and repetitive of material in C. O. 217 and Cape Breton B.

The even briefer Colonial Office 221, Volumes 34-35, contain shipping returns for Cape Breton, 1785-1815. These are an important aid in analyzing the true economic state of the island under DesBarres' administration. Similar shipping returns for Prince Edward Island, 1807-1809, will be found in C. O. 231, Volume 2. In the much larger Colonial Office 5, America and West Indies, Volume 7 contains the estimates of the cost of surveys in North America, 1764-1776, Volume 67 has a statement by the Board of Trade regarding the coal mines on Cape Breton, 1766, and Volume 68 contains Holland's survey of Cape Breton, 1766-1767, together with a statement of his expenses, 1765-1767. Letters to Holland concerning his surveys will be found in Volumes 243-245.

The author used the copies of the Colonial Office papers which are available at the Public Archives of Canada. The Archives has only had copies made of those items relating to North America. They have been brought together as Manuscript Group 11, for which a general inventory was published in 1961. In this Group, Supplementary II, Item 2, contains the commission for Walter Patterson as Governor of the island of St. John. The commission to Governor Parr of Nova Scotia will be found in Item 12, his instructions in Item 13 of the same section. The commissions and instructions for DesBarres' administration in Cape Breton are in Item 14 and those for Prince Edward Island in Item 17. Papers relating to the alteration of land instructions in Prince Edward Island, 1806, will be found in Supplementary I, Item 27. Of the papers in PAC, Record Group 8: British Military and Naval Records, only a few isolated papers useful for this study were found in Records of the Nova Scotia Command, 1762-1899, Volumes 1425 and 1426; Ordnance Records: Reports and Returns, 1757-1878, Volume 89. An inventory of this group was published in 1954 by the Archives. Hardly one paper mentioning DesBarres by name was discovered in the several volumes examined, a reflection of his comparative obscurity before 1764 and his indeterminate position thereafter.

3. *Other Manuscripts*

Six large sets of papers offered important material for this study. The PAC has transcribed parts of the Shelburne Papers (MG 23, A. 3). Volumes 9-11 have been calendared in *Report* of the Public Archives for 1912, the remainder in the *Report* for 1921. For this study, material was found in Volumes 53, 55-56, 67-69, 111.

Another valuable group is the Dartmouth Papers, mainly those of William Legge, 2d Earl of Dartmouth (MG 23, A. 1). The copies of these papers in the possession of the PAC are: (a) restricted to those of North American interest, and (b) in three overlapping series. The first group consists of original documents, Series I, acquired in 1926. The second group contains transcripts M383-385B and M650, which are copies of those documents in *Report* of the Historical Manuscripts Commission of Great Britain, Number 14, Appendix 10 (1895). A third group consists of transcripts of documents from Patshull House, Wolverhampton, England. These papers were calendared in the *Report* of the Hist. MSS Comm., Number 10, Appendix 5 (1887). For this study Series I, containing material on all aspects of Nova Scotia history during the eighteenth century, was useful. Particularly valuable is the economic data. Volume 12 of this first series has papers relevant to the history of Prince Edward Island, 1766-1776. Series 2. Transcripts M383-385B, M650, covering the period 1757-1792, is of less value but Series 3, Patshull transcripts, contains much information on Nova Scotia before 1784.

For the history of Prince Edward Island in the first years of the nineteenth century, the Selkirk Papers (MG 19, E. 1) possess an enormous body of information, especially on economic matters. The Selkirk settlement in Prince Edward is dealt with in Volumes 56, 59, 73, 74, 77, and 78. Volume 74 also contains that part of Selkirk's diary which relates to his visit to the island. The diary has been edited by Patrick C. White (Toronto, 1958). The Selkirk Papers present the most detailed and most reliable extragovernmental source of information on the condition of the island immediately prior to DesBarres' arrival.

A less well-known group of documents is the Inglis Papers (MG 23, C. 6). The bulk of these are the journals, papers, and letters of Charles Inglis, first Bishop of Nova Scotia. Inglis had little to say directly concerning matters in Cape Breton, but he presented interesting details and insights regarding Nova Scotia's economy and politics, as well as its religious life, for the period of DesBarres' administration in the island. Of particular interest for this study were Volume 1, letters sent by Inglis, 1787-1791 and Volume 4, the journal of John Inglis, the son who became third Bishop of Nova Scotia in 1825.

The extensive American Headquarters Papers, also known as the Carleton Papers (MG 23, B. 1) proved somewhat disappointing. These papers contain selections from the correspondence of the Commanders in Chief, Sir William Howe, 1775-1779, Sir Henry Clinton, 1778-1783, Sir Guy Carleton, 1782-1783, and their secretaries. A calendar was published by the Historical Manuscripts Commission of Great Britain in 1904. There are a large number of items dealing with Prince Edward Island and Nova Scotia, but they are for the period prior to DesBarres' administration in Cape Breton. There is also a considerable body of material dealing with the migration of the Loyalists to Nova Scotia and New Brunswick, but almost no mention of the smaller movement to Cape Breton. The volumes which did contain material useful for this study were: 11, 16, 21, 29, 52.

For the settlement of the Loyalists in Cape Breton the most valuable group of private documents, in addition to those of DesBarres, were the Haldimand Papers (MG 21, G. 2). They are arranged in 232 volumes. A general guide, by volume, will be found in David W. Parker, *A Guide to the Documents in the Manuscript Room at the Public Archives of Canada* (Ottawa, 1914), pp. 199-210. A calendar of the collection was published in *Reports* of the PAC 1884-1889. Volume 165 and, to a lesser extent, Volumes 166-168 are the relevant sections for this study. The Haldimand Papers, whose originals are in the British Museum, contain a wealth of information on one of the most successful members of the Royal American Regiment. A scholarly life of Haldimand is needed.

Exhaustive inquiries failed to reveal any other important group of papers which demonstrated the character and policies of Abraham Cuyler, who served Haldimand before going to Cape Breton. A few letters in the New-York Historical Society and the Historical Society of Pennsylvania deal with his business affairs, but they are not sufficiently complete to provide much insight into the extent and character of his trading activities. Inquiries at other New York depositories, from state to parish level, did not turn up any further papers.

For Cuyler's principal supporter, David Mathews, no more could be found that a few form letters in the Gratz Collection, Historical Society of Pennsylvania and Miscellaneous MSS D, E, M, and R in the New-York Historical Society.

In addition to these large collections, smaller groups of manuscripts proved valuable for certain matters. At the Public Archives of Nova Scotia a few items not found in the Colonial Office records or the DesBarres Papers were seen in Volumes 315, 333, 344, 394, 430, 443, and 458. These volumes may be used only with a card index at the archives. Calendars have not been published, except for special collections, such as that of Margaret Ells, comp., *A Calendar of the White Collection of Manuscripts in the Public Archives* ("P. A. N. S. Publication," No. 5, Halifax, 1940).

In the papers of the Rev. Andrew Brown (PAC, MG 21, E. 5) which were gathered together about 1791 for a history of Nova Scotia, are pieces of information not found elsewhere. The originals are in the British Museum, Add. MSS 19069-19076. Manuscript 19071, f. 233-238 contains a brief sketch of Nova Scotia by Judge Isaac Deschamps; MS 19073, f. 116-125 contains notes on the Acadians by Joseph Gray, who served as an agent for DesBarres, and f. 126-135 holds "Observations on agriculture in Nova Scotia" by Moses Delesdernier, with whom DesBarres had several commercial and legal transactions. The draft history by Brown, MSS 19075-19076 is hardly legible but appears to proceed no further than 1766. It is briefly discussed by Charles B. Fergusson, *The Public Archives of Nova Scotia* ("P. A. N. S. Bulletin," No. 19, Halifax, 1963), pp. 7-8.

On the problems of Nova Scotia land utilization, and as background to an analysis of the DesBarres estates, the author utilized material in the Ball Estate-Dupuy Papers and the Hughes Papers at the Historical Society of Pennsylvania. These show the interest of American investors in Nova Scotia in the 1760's. The abstract of land grants, 1732-1864, arranged by Nova Scotia counties (MG 9, B. 5) was of very limited value. Margaret Gilroy, comp., *Loyalists and Land Settlement in Nova Scotia* ("P. A. N. S. Publication," No. 4, Halifax, 1937) is simply a listing of land grants. Cape Breton was not included in its coverage.

The first years of Loyalist settlement in Cape Breton are described in chapter IV of this work. In order to have comparative material the author examined the Botsford Papers (MG 23, D. 4), the Chatham Papers (PAC transcripts, MG 23, A. 2), Volumes 343-344, brief transcripts from the papers of Thomas Townshend, 1st Viscount Sydney (MG 23, B. 3), the Dartmouth Papers, especially Series I, Volumes 3-4, and the White Collection at the PANS. There is a need for a scholarly history of the Loyalists in Nova Scotia based upon these materials, the Shelburne newspapers (copies at PANS), land grant papers at the PANS, and the Colonial Office records.

MAPS AND CHARTS

THE following listing may not be exhaustive but it certainly includes the vast majority of those depositories having one or more copies of the *Atlantic Neptune*. In the United States there are copies at *American Geographical Society, New York City; Boston Athenaeum; *Boston Public Library; Charleston Library Society, Charleston, South Carolina; Harvard College Library; Henry E. Huntington Library, San Marino, California; *John Carter Brown Library, Providence, Rhode Island; Library of Congress; *Newberry Library, Chicago; *New-York Historical Society, *New York Public Library; *Mariners Museum, Newport News, Virginia; Peabody Museum, Salem, Massachusetts; U. S. Naval Academy Library, Annapolis, Maryland; William L. Clements Library, Ann Arbor, Michigan; *Yale University Library.

* Copies seen by the author.

Bibliographical Essay

In the United Kingdom, copies are held by the Admiralty Archives; Bodleian Library, Oxford University; the British Museum; and the National Maritime Museum, Greenwich (Stevens Collection).*

In Canada, *Neptunes* may be seen at the Public Archives of Canada, Ottawa* (copy of Jeffrey Amherst); Public Archives of Nova Scotia*; the New Brunswick Museum (Webster Canadiana Collection), and the Legislative Library of New Brunswick.*

There is also a copy at the Bibliothèque National in Paris.

While the above listing will provide many readers with an opportunity to view the delicate delights of DesBarres' great work, those not near the depositories may be interested in the substantive reproduction of the *Neptune* now being issued by the Barre Press.

Copies of the partial catalogue which DesBarres published as *Surveys of North America, entitled "Atlantic Neptune"; published by command of government for the use of the Royal Navy of Great-Britain* (London, W. Babbs, 1781) are available in the Harvard College Library and the Library of Congress. A photostat of the latter may be seen at the New York Public Library. Other catalogues which give descriptions of the *Neptune* are:

Obadiah Rich, *Bibiotheca Americana Nova* (2 vols.; London, 1835) I, 249-51.

Philip L. Phillips, *A List of Geographical Atlases in the Library of Congress* (6 vols.; Washington, 1909-1963) I, 632-54; III, 453-71; IV, 253-57.

Robert Lingel, "The Atlantic Neptune," *Bulletin of the New York Public Library*, XL (1936), 581-603.

John C. Webster, comp., *Catalogue of the John Clarence Webster Canadiana Collection, New Brunswick Museum* (3 vols.; Saint John, N. B., 1938-1959). The collection is briefly described by Arthur G. Bailey, *The John Clarence Webster Collection* ("New Brunswick Museum Collections," No. 1, Saint John, N. B., 1936).

The PANS copies are listed in Marion Gilroy, comp., *A Catalogue of Maps, Plans and Charts in the Public Archives of Nova Scotia* ("P. A. N. S. Bulletin," I, No. 3, Halifax, 1938).

Bernard Quaritch Ltd., London, *Catalogue* No. 281 (1909), pp. 10-12; 438 (1930), pp. 1-6; 520 (1936), pp. 1-7.

The British Museum, *Catalogue of Maps, Prints, Drawings, etc. form-*

* Copies seen by the author.

ing the Geographical and Topographical Collection attached to the Library of His Late Majesty King George the Third (London, 1829) contains no entry for the *Neptune,* and British Museum, *Catalogue of the printed Maps, Plans, and Charts in the British Museum* (2 vols.; London, 1885) has only a simple entry without an analysis of contents.

The author found it profitable to examine maps and charts contemporary with those of DesBarres at all the depositories he visited, for example those of Jacques Nicolas Bellin at the New York Public Library and Yale University. In this way a grasp of the state of the art in the 1760's came as a result of direct observation, and it was possible to evaluate DesBarres' work in the light of contemporary failures and achievements.

The shortage of evidence regarding DesBarres' hydrographic methods placed a premium upon such printed contemporary works as those of Murdoch Mackenzie, which are discussed below. American treatises on marine surveying are nearly all from the post-Revolutionary period and therefore of limited value for this study. One of the most interesting is Robert Patterson's treatise on navigation (1789) in the Historical Society of Pennsylvania. But few materials in this field are in manuscript, since the compilation of atlases and books of charts had the obvious object of utility. Nearly all which have survived will be found in printed form. Treatises on marine surveying were much less common in the eighteenth century than books of instruction for land surveyors. Neither totaled more than a fraction of the maps and charts drawn up on the principles they propounded.

PRINTED SOURCES

Of DesBarres' acknowledged works only the *Atlantic Neptune* and *A Statement submitted by Lieutenant Colonel DesBarres, for Consideration. Respecting his services ... during the war of 1756. The utility of his surveys and publications of the coasts and harbours of North America, intituled, The Atlantic Neptune.—and his proceedings and conduct as Lieutenant Governor ... of Cape Breton* (London, 1795) have been published.

Robert Harrison in his article on DesBarres in the *Dictionary of National Biography* declares that a book on Cape Breton was privately printed by him in London in 1804 but that it was suppressed. This statement may have been based on Entry 623 in the *Catalogue of Books relating to America, in the Collection of Colonel Aspinwall* (Paris? 1832?). DesBarres' authorship is also noted in S. Austin Allibone, *A Critical Dictionary of English Literature* (5 vols.; Philadelphia, 1900), with a reference to the Aspinwall catalogue. Interestingly, no mention of the work is made in *The English Catalogue of Books,* in Robert Watt's *Bibliotheca Britannica,* in the *Cambridge Bibliography of English Literature,* in the *Subject Catalogue of the Library of the Royal Empire Society* or in the British Museum, *Catalogue of Printed Books.*

Nevertheless, such a work was definitely published. Internal evidence makes it absolutely clear that DesBarres was the author of *Letters to Lord * * * * * on a Caveat against Emigration to America with the State of the Island of Cape Breton, from the Year 1784 to the Present Year . . .* (London, 1804). The author of *A Caveat* (London, 1803) was William Smith who had served as surgeon on the island during DesBarres' governorship. The *Letters,* which stretches to two hundred and twenty-eight printed pages, combines a staunch defense of DesBarres' policies with sarcastic attacks on his opponents. The rarity of the work may account for its neglect by the colony's historians. Yet it remains not only one of the most coherent statements of DesBarres' views on imperial policies but also an analysis of his administration which, while not entirely convincing, certainly commands our attention.

A letter from DesBarres to Lord George Germaine, October 1, 1779, which analyzes the "utility of Nova Scotia" has been printed in William I. Morse (ed.), *Acadiensia Nova, 1598-1779* (2 vols.; London, 1935) II, 105-21. The original may be seen in the Morse collection, Dalhousie University.

The following relevant parts of the official documents for Prince Edward Island have been published: *Journal of the House of Assembly of His Majesty's Island of Saint John,* 1804-1808 and *Journal of His Majesty's Island of Prince Edward,* 1809-1812. The journals of the Council were not printed until 1827. The *Statutes* of the island were published each year except between 1798 and 1805 when the island was without a King's printer. Copies of these documents are not easily available and it may be easier to consult those contained in the appropriate Colonial Office series. For the unpublished Cape Breton documents this is essential. A useful guide is Olga B. Bishop, *Publications of the Governments of Nova Scotia, Prince Edward Island, New Brunswick, 1758-1952* (Ottawa, 1957).

Chapter II

DesBarres' *Atlantic Neptune* is the key printed work for a discussion of his hydrographical achievements. The charts and maps of Holland, Bellin, and others can also be seen at the depositories mentioned above.

Murdoch Mackenzie, *Orcades: or a Geographic and Hydrographic Survey of the Orkney and Lewis Islands* (London, 1750; 3d rev. ed., 1776, used) was a valuable work whose precepts coincided well with DesBarres' practices. Another work of special interest was William Gerard DeBrahm, *The Levelling Balance and Counter-Balance* (London, 1774). Mackenzie's *Treatise on Marine Surveying* (London, 1774) was the most sophisticated discussion in English to appear during DesBarres' period of surveying and chart making. A large number of articles on land and marine surveying by such scientists as John Hadley and Edmund Halley will be found in the *Philosophical Transactions* of the Royal Society of London for the period c. 1740-c. 1775.

The development of the art of map making may be seen in such works as:

Armando Cortesa Da Mota (ed.), *Portugaliae Monumenta Cartographica* (4 vols.; Lisbon, 1960).

Anthony Ashley, *The Mariner's Mirror* (London, 1588).

Robert Dudley, *Arcano Del Mare* (2 vols.; Firenze, 1646-1647).

Greenvile Collins, *Great Britain's Coasting Pilot* (London, 1693; edition used, London, 1776).

Four representative examples of mid-eighteenth-century discourses on cartography are:

John Green, *Remarks, in Support of the New Chart of North and South America* (London, 1753).

Joseph Bernard, Marquis de Chabert de Cogolin, *Voyage fait par Ordre du Roi en 1750 et 1751, dans L'Amérique Septentrionale* (Paris, 1753).

Lewis Evans' essay on his famous map of the middle British colonies in *Geographical, Historical, Political, Philosophical and Mechanical Essays* (Philadelphia, 1755).

Explanation for the New Map of Nova Scotia and Cape Breton with the Adjacent Parts of New England and Canada (London, 1755), which probably was the work of its printer, Thomas Jefferys, but may have been written by John Green.

The works of Jacques Nicolas Bellin are of considerable importance for this study, because they reveal the state of French hydrography in the decade immediately preceding DesBarres' work. A most interesting work, which shows similarities with the *Atlantic Neptune*, is *Le Petit Atlas Maritime Recueil De Cartes et Plans Des Quartre Parties du Monde* (5 vols.; Paris? 1764). North America and the West Indies are covered in Volume

Bibliographical Essay

I. A selection of Bellin's maps, charts, and plans has been reproduced in *Old Maps of the World* (5 vols.; Cleveland, 1959), issued by Bloch & Company. The North American group consists entirely of maps originally printed in 1757. Bellin's maps were used in Pierre Charlevoix, *Histoire et Description Generale de la Nouvelle France* (3 vols.; Paris, 1744), in Paul U. Du Buisson, *Storia della Rivoluzione dell' America inglese* (3 vols.; Venice, 1782-1784). Volumes I and II are a translation, probably by the publisher V. A. Formaleoni, of Du Buisson's *Abrégé de la Révolution de l'Amérique Angloise*. Bellin's maps were also used in the famous *Histoire Générale des Voyages* (20 vols.; Paris and Amsterdam, 1746-1770) compiled by Antoine François Prévost.

The Dispatches of Rear-Admiral Lord Colville 1759-1761 ("Maritime Museum of Canada, Occasional Papers," No. 4, Halifax, 1958), and *The Recapture of St. John's Newfoundland* ("Maritime Museum of Canada, Occasional Papers," No. 6, Halifax, 1959), are brief selections in which one might expect to find a reference to DesBarres. None occurs.

Chapter IV

In addition to the writings of Samuel Holland and William Smith already mentioned, there exist three other valuable descriptions of Cape Breton which are roughly contemporaneous with DesBarres' administration. In chronological order they are:

Thomas Pichon, *Lettres et Memoires pour servir a l'Histoire du Cap Breton* (London, 1760).

Samuel W. Prenties, *Narrative of a Shipwreck on the Island of Cape Breton in a Voyage from Quebec, 1780* (London, 1783).

Charles B. Fergusson (ed.), *Uniacke's Sketches of Cape Breton and Other Papers relating to Cape Breton Island* ("P. A. N. S., Nova Scotia series," Halifax, 1958). Contains three brief accounts of Sydney in 1785, 1788, and 1789.

Chapter V

The only printed source used for this chapter was DesBarres' *Statement respecting his Services* (1795).

Chapter VI

Prince Edward Island received much more attention from travelers than did Cape Breton Island. The quitrent issue was sufficiently emotional and important to guarantee local persons with a literary bent an audience, once they mentioned the island's land problems. The following works provided glimpses of Prince Edward Island before and during DesBarres' administration. They are listed in chronological order:

Census and Report of Sieur de la Roque (1752) reproduced in translation in *Report Concerning Canadian Archives for the Year 1905* (Ottawa, 1906), II, Appendix A, 76-165.

"Orders in Council (Imperial): Land Grants in Prince Edward Island, 1767" reproduced in *Report Concerning Canadian Archives for the Year 1905* (Ottawa, 1906), I, Part 2, 12-22.

Daniel C. Harvey, *Journeys to the Island of St. John; or Prince Edward Island, 1775-1832* (Toronto, 1955). Includes the narrative of Curtis (1775).

Patrick M'Robert, *A Tour through Part of the North Provinces of America* (Edinburgh, 1776). This work has also been reprinted in Historical Society of Pennsylvania, *Pamphlet Series*, No. 1 (1935).

Lord Selkirk's Diary, 1803-1804, ed. Patrick C. T. White ("Publications of the Champlain Society," No. 35, Toronto, 1958).

Anon., *General Idea of the Qualities of Prince Edward Island and of an Estate which is to be sold there* . . . (London, 1804). Very good account of Macdonald's "Tracadie" estate.

Thomas Douglas, 5th Earl of Selkirk, *Observations on the Present State of the Highlands* . . . (London, 1805), especially pp. 189-219, which cover the settlement on Prince Edward Island.

John Stewart, *An Account of Prince Edward Island in the Gulph of St. Lawrence* (London, 1806). A lengthy and detailed narrative whose interpretations reflect the author's partisan position in the island's political life.

Joseph O. Plessis, *Voyages dans le Golfe Saint Laurent et les Provinces D'en Bas, en 1811 et 1812*, in *Le Foyer Canadien Recueil Litteraire et Historique*, III (Mai-Novembre, 1865), 190-202. This includes notes of an interview with John Macdonald, and a description of Charlottetown.

Facts versus Lord Durham: Remarks upon that Portion of the Earl of Durham's Report Relating to Prince Edward Island, showing the Fallacy of the Statements contained Therein . . . by a Proprietor (London, 1839). One of the best presentations of the proprietors' case.

BIBLIOGRAPHICAL AIDS

In addition to the customary bibliographical aids, such as the *Harvard Guide to American History*, the following works of a more specialized nature were of particular value to the author. They are listed in alphabetical order:

Robert G. Albion, *Maritime and Naval History: An Annotated Bibliography* (rev. ed.; Mystic, Conn., 1955).

Eugenie Archibald, comp., *Catalogue of the William Inglis Morse Collection at Dalhousie University Library* (London, 1938).

Olga B. Bishop, *Publications of the Governments of Nova Scotia, Prince Edward Island, New Brunswick, 1758-1952* (Ottawa, 1957).

Canada, Dept. of Mines and Technical Surveys, Geographical Branch, *Bibliography of Periodical Literature on Canadian Geography, 1930-1955* ("Dept. of Mines, Bibliographical Series," No. 22, Ottawa, 1959), Part 2 relevant.

Ibid., *Colonization and Land Settlement in the Americas: A Selected Bibliography* ("Bibliographical Series," No. 25, Ottawa, 1960), pp. 5-15.

Edward G. Cox, *A Reference Guide to the Literature of Travel, Volume II: The New World* ("University of Washington Publications in Language and Literature," No. 10, Seattle, 1938).

Hardin Craig, Jr., *A Bibliography of Encyclopaedias and Dictionaries dealing with Military, Naval and Maritime Affairs, 1577-1961* (mimeographed, Fondren Library, Rice University, Houston, 1962). An invaluable aid for the examination or clarification of technical matters from a *historical* standpoint.

Narcisse E. Dionne, *Inventaire Chronologique des Cartes, Plans* constitutes the fourth volume in his *Bibliographie Canadienne* (5 vols.; Quebec, 1905-1909).

Chauncey D. Harris and Jerome D. Fellmann, *A Union List of Geographical Serials* (2d ed.; Chicago, 1954), and *International List of Geographical Serials* ("University of Chicago, Dept. of Geog., Research Paper," No. 63, Chicago, 1960).

Library of Congress, Map Division, *A Guide to Historical Cartography* (2d rev. ed.; Washington, 1960); is a brief selection by Walter W. Ristow of introductory works covering the whole field.

William Mathews, *Canadian Diaries and Autobiographies* (Berkeley, Calif., 1950).

Public Archives of Canada, *Catalogue of Maps, Plans, and Charts in the Map Room of the Dominion Archives* (Ottawa, 1912) and *Sixteenth-Century Maps Relating to Canada; a Check-List and Bibliography* (Ottawa, 1956).

Frances M. Staton and Marie Tremaine, *A Bibliography of Canadiana* (Toronto, 1934).

Raymond Tanghe, *Bibliography of Canadian Bibliographies* (Toronto, 1960).

University of Michigan, William L. Clements Library, *An Exhibition of Maps Engraved within the Present Limits of the United States mostly prior to 1800* (Ann Arbor, 1933). Contains a succinct account of the first map engraved on copper (1683), John Norman's *American Pilot* (1792), Joshua Fisher's chart of Delaware Bay (1731) and Benjamin Franklin's chart of the Gulf Stream (1786).

Francisco Vindel, *Mapas de America en Los Libros de Los Siglos XVI al XVIII* (Madrid, 1955).

Reginald E. Watters, *A Check List of Canadian Literature and Background Materials, 1628-1950* (Toronto, 1959).

John K. Wright and Elizabeth T. Platt, *Aids to Geographical Research* ("American Geographical Society, Research Series," No. 22, 2d rev. ed.; New York, 1947).

SELECTED SECONDARY WORKS

JOHN C. WEBSTER, *The Life of Joseph Frederick Wallet DesBarres* (privately printed, Shediac, N. B., 1933) and "Joseph Frederick Wallet DesBarres and the Atlantic Neptune," *Transactions,* Roy. Soc. of Canada, 3d Ser., XXI (1927), sec. 2, 21-41, are the only previous accounts of DesBarres' careers which require consideration. There are one or two other, very brief articles about DesBarres in minor publications but these are based on Webster's work. There were two central weaknesses in his examination of DesBarres' life. Firstly, he tended to be too ready to accept DesBarres' estimates of men and situations. Secondly, he had only a small proportion of the total DesBarres Papers on which to base his account.

The outline of the story, as presented by Webster, is accurate. But the great quantity of new material, the extensive use of the Colonial Office records, and evidence from other private papers modifies his conclusions in a number of important areas. This is particularly true for DesBarres' two administrations and the management of his estates.

It must be emphasized that the following notes are highly selective in their nature. No attempt has been made to list the total number of works consulted. The technical character of many of the topics dealt with demanded that the author master the details of such matters as portolan charts, marine surveying, and eighteenth-century land law. Each historian will pursue his own method of acquiring this type of knowledge; it is hoped that the bibliographical aids listed above will be of value.

Introduction

Lewis W. G. Butler, *The Annals of the King's Royal Rifle Corps* (5 vols.; London, 1913).

Louis des Cognets, *Amherst and Canada* (privately printed, 1962) claims to be based on manuscript sources but its lack of references makes it an annoying and unreliable work.

Oliver F. G. Hogg, *The Royal Arsenal* (2 vols.; London, 1963). A new study which promises to be definitive.

Whitworth Porter, *History of the Corps of Engineers* (2 vols.; London, 1889).

George F. G. Stanley, *Canada's Soldiers: The Military History of an Unmilitary People* (rev. ed.; Toronto, 1960).

Chapter II

Neither the famous old work, Alfred T. Mahan, *The Major Operations of the Navies in the War of American Independence* (Boston, 1913) nor the excellent new study, Piers Mackesy, *The War for America, 1775-1783* (Cambridge, Mass., 1964) pays sufficient attention to the questions of pilots and charts.

Three useful general studies in the history of British hydrography, a much neglected field:

Mary Blewitt, *Surveys of the Seas* (London, 1957). No mention of DesBarres.

Adrian H. W. Robinson, *Marine Cartography in Britain: A History of the Sea Chart to 1855* (Leicester, Eng., 1962). This is an excellently organized work which throws interesting light on the map and chart trade in DesBarres' day.

George S. Ritchie, *The Admiralty Chart: British Naval Hydrography in the Nineteenth Century* (London, 1967). DesBarres is mentioned three times. Chapters 1 and 2 are relevant. Ritchie relies heavily on Webster.

A disappointing work, because it confines itself merely to listing individuals and companies, is Charles E. Smart, *The Makers of Surveying Instruments in America since 1700* (Troy, N. Y., 1962).

The literature on copyright law and its history is very large. A convenient guide is Henriette Mertz, *Copyright Bibliography* (Washington, 1950). Augustine Birrell, *Seven Lectures on the Law and History of Copyright in Books* (New York, 1899) has not been equalled in its combination of literary elegance and sure grasp of the values involved. Historical summaries covering most of the period of DesBarres' publishing activity are Arthur S. Collins, "Some Aspects of Copyright from 1700 to 1780," *The Library*, 4th Series, VII (1927), 67-81 and Alfred W. Pollard, "Some Notes on the History of Copyright in England, 1662-1774," *ibid.*, III (1922), 97-114. A work whose range is broader than most studies is Thomas E. Scrutton, *The Laws of Copyright* (London, 1882). This, together with eighteenth-century pamphlets and the other secondary works cited here, clearly reveal the lack of legislation covering charts and engravings during DesBarres' career.

J. H. Broomfield, "Lord Sandwich at the Admiralty Board: Politics and the Navy Board, 1771-1778." *The Mariner's Mirror*, LI (1965), 7-17, Allan Fraser, "The Recapture of Saint John's, September, 1762," *Atlantic Advocate*, LVI (April, 1968), 42-47, and Neil R. Stout "Manning the Royal Navy in North America, 1763-1775," *American Neptune*, XXIII (July, 1963), 174-85 are three articles with useful background information.

Chapter III

George T. Bates "John Goreham, 1709-1751," *Collections*, Nova Scotia Hist. Soc., XXX (1954). Information on the Goreham family, suggestive of connections with DesBarres.

Winthrop P. Bell, *The "Foreign Protestants" and the Settlement of Nova Scotia* (Toronto, 1961). Breaks new ground. Its value diminished by its poor notes on manuscript sources and a highly personal format.

Beverly W. Bond, *The Quit-Rent System in the American Colonies* ("Yale Historical Publications," Misc. VI, New Haven, 1919).

Arthur W. Eaton "Rhode Island Settlers on the French Lands in Nova Scotia in 1760 and 1761," *Americana*, X (1915), and "The Settling of

Colchester County, Nova Scotia," *Transactions*, Roy. Soc. of Canada, 3d Ser., VI (1912), Sec. II, 221-65.

Marshall Harris, *Origin of the Land Tenure System in the United States* (Ames, Iowa, 1953). Concentrates on the colonial and early national period.

William S. Holdsworth, *An Historical Introduction to the Land Law* (Oxford, 1917). The best starting point.

James S. Macdonald "Memoir, Lieut.-Governor Michael Francklin 1752-1782," *Collections*, Nova Scotia Hist. Soc., XVI (1912).

Norman Macdonald, *Canada, 1763-1841, Immigration and Land Settlement: The Administration of the Imperial Land Regulations* (London, 1939). Indispensable. Stands alone in its field. A balanced treatment although the author is sometimes a little too ready to condemn the "gross ignorance of colonial conditions and needs." Summary of his conclusions in *Land Tenure on the North American Continent* ("Toronto University Studies in History and Economics," VII, 1934), 21-44.

William S. McNutt, *New Brunswick, A History: 1784-1807* (Toronto, 1963).

William C. Milner, *The Basin of Minas and its Early Settlers* (Wolfville, N. S., 193-?). Reproduction of a number of newspaper articles. The essay on DesBarres' estates is brief, untechnical and inaccurate.

Frank H. Patterson, *A History of Tatamagouche, Nova Scotia* (Halifax, 1917). The only history available; to be used with care.

George Patterson, *History of the County of Pictou* (Montreal, 1887). Also to be used with caution.

Esther C. Wright, *The Petitcodiac* (Sackville, N. B., 1945). Weak in handling technical problems connected with land tenures. Undocumented.

Chapter IV

James Murray Beck, *The Government of Nova Scotia* ("Canadian Government Series" No. 8, Toronto, 1957). Weak on historical aspects.

John G. Bourinot, *Historical and Descriptive Account of the Island of Cape Breton* (Montreal, 1892). A solid history, in many ways superior to the work usually read, Richard Brown, *A History of the Island of Cape Breton* (London, 1869).

Ella H. Cameron "Imperial Policy in Cape Breton, 1784-1795," *Collections*, Nova Scotia Hist. Soc. XXXI (1957). Failure to use the Des-

Barres Papers and other MSS sources makes this less than a definitive study.

The *Cape Breton Mirror* which was published monthly, December 1951 to December 1953, is of no value to scholars of the island's history. Whatever historical notes it contains are found elsewhere in more reliable form.

Cape Breton Historical Society, *Papers* (1928-1932). This short-lived series contains little other than notes of local interest.

John Doull, "The First Five Attorney-Generals of Nova Scotia," *Collections*, Nova Scotia Hist. Soc., XXVI (1945), 33-48. Information on Richard Gibbons.

Marion Gilroy "The Partition of Nova Scotia," *Canadian Historical Review*, XIV (1933), 375-91. An important article whose conclusion, that the partition was the result of major policy changes by the imperial government, is not fully convincing.

Gerald S. Graham, *British Policy and Canada, 1774-1791: A Study in Eighteenth Century Trade Policy* (London, 1930) and *Empire of the North Atlantic: The Maritime Struggle for North America* (2d ed.; Toronto, 1958).

A. H. McLintock, *The Establishment of Constitutional Government in Newfoundland, 1783-1832* (London, 1941).

Chapter VI

J. B. Bird, "Settlement Patterns in Maritime Canada, 1687-1786" *Geographical Review*, XLV (1955), 385-404.

Lorne C. Callbeck, The *Cradle of Confederation* (Fredericton, N. B., 1964). Does not fill the need for a scholarly history of Prince Edward Island since 1767.

Andrew A. Clark, *Three Centuries and the Island* (Toronto, 1959). An excellent historical geography.

Helen I. Cowan, *British Emigration to British North America, 1783-1857* (Toronto, 1928), chaps. I and II.

Daniel C. Harvey, *The French Regime in Prince Edward Island* (New Haven, 1926).

Frank J. MacKinnon, *The Government of Prince Edward Island* (Toronto, 1951).

Bibliographical Essay

Wilbur H. Siebert and Florence E. Gilliam, *The Loyalists in Prince Edward Island* (Ottawa, 1911).

Ada P. McLeod, *The Selkirk Settlers and the Church they Built at Belfast* (Toronto, 1939).

Alexander B. Warburton, *A History of Prince Edward Island* (Saint John, N. B., 1923). Based on use of official records, but unscholarly in style. Often fails to distinguish between quotations from sources and the author's own words. Does not deal with the period after 1831.

INDEX

Index

Index

Index

35, 40; in Cape Breton, 45, 55; in Prince Edward Island, 80-81

Landholding, and military officers, 27; fees in Nova Scotia, 28; purchase prices, 32-33; profitability of, 35-39; rents, 35 n.; by lottery, 80; proprietors (Prince Edward Island), 80-83

Lawsuits, DesBarres with tenants, viii, 34, 38-39, 40-41; with merchants, 34

Lawyers, employed by DesBarres, 39, 40-41

Louisbourg, Cape Breton, 7

Loyal Electors, Society of, 90, 92-93

Loyalists, *see* American Loyalists.

Maccan-Nappan, DesBarres estate, 27, 30, 31

Macdonald, John (Captain), reports on DesBarres estates, 31 n., 36-37

Machias, Maine, expedition from, 32

Mackenzie, Murdock (the elder), 10; comments on surveying, 15; and Admiralty, 67

Mackworth, Herbert (Sir), 73, 75, 78

Maillard, Peter, complains re rents, 35

Mariner's Mirror (1588), 10

Maskelyne, Nevil (Astronomer Royal), 11

Mathematics, history, 4

Mathews, David, 46, 52, 72

Memramcook-Petitcodiac, DesBarres estate, 27, 32 n.

Mercenaries, in British Army, 6

Minudie, DesBarres estate, 27, 30

Montbéliard, county of, 3, 31

Montréal, 8

Morris, Charles, Sr., 34, 39

Morris, Charles, Jr., 39

Nautical Remarks and Observations . . . Nova Scotia (DesBarres), 20

Navigation, aids to, 9-10, 15; instruments for, 63

Nepean, Evan (undersecretary), 48, 73

Newfoundland, 8

Newport, R. I., town plan, 25

Nova Scotia, maps of, 16-17; charts of, 17-21; economy of, 30, 35; government of, 45-46

Octant, 9

Odell, Jonathan, 41 n.

Oldmixon, John, estimate of Cape Breton, 69

Owen, William F., surveys New Brunswick, 25

Palmer, James, 89, 90, 92

Parker, Hyde (1739-1807), 24

Parr, John, 46, 51

Patterson, Walter, 80-81, 84, 85

Perceval, John (Earl of Egmont), 80

Philadelphia Company, lands in Nova Scotia, 29

Pipes, William, 31

President (vessel), 52

Prevost, Augustine, 7

Prevost, James, 6, 7

Prince Edward Island, Holland surveys, 12, 25, 80; in *Atlantic Neptune*, 21; French settlement, 79-80; estimates of, 79-81; population (1752), 79; land grants, 80-81; quitrents, 80-81, 83, 89, 91; militia, 84, 86; postal service, 84; roads, 84-87, 89; public buildings, 86, 89

Rents, 35 n., 36

[129]

Index